STRETCHING THE SOUL

Also by Ron Wilson

You Can Be a Point of Light
A Flower Grows in Ireland
Adventure of the Iron Camels
Lost in the Shenandoahs
The C.B. Mystery

STRETCHING THE SOUL

Learning the Art of Watching God Work

Ronald E. Wilson

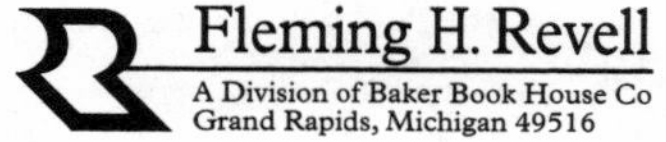
Fleming H. Revell
A Division of Baker Book House Co
Grand Rapids, Michigan 49516

© 1995 by Ronald E. Wilson

Published by Fleming H. Revell
a division of Baker Book House Company
P.O. Box 6287, Grand Rapids, MI 49516-6287

Printed in the United States of America

All rights reserved. No part of this publication may be reproduced, stored in a retrieval system, or transmitted in any form or by any means—for example electronic, photocopy, recording—without the prior written permission of the publisher. The only exception is brief quotations in printed reviews.

Library of Congress Cataloging-in-Publication Data

Wilson, Ron, 1932—
Stretching the soul : learning the art of watching God work / Ronald E. Wilson
p. cm.
ISBN 0-8007-5554-5
1. Wilson, Ron, 1932— . 2. Remarried people—Biography. 3. Remarried people—Religous life. 4. Spiritual biography. I. Title
BV4439.W55 1995
248.8'425—dc20 94-39930

Unless otherwise marked, Scripture quotations are taken from the HOLY BIBLE, NEW INTERNATIONAL VERSION ®. NIV ®. Copyright © 1973, 1978, 1984 by International Bible Society. Used by permission of Zondervan Publishing House. All rights reserved.

Scripture marked NEB is taken from *The New English Bible*. © The Delegates of the Oxford University Press and The Syndics of the Cambridge University Press 1961, 1970. Reprinted by permission.

Scripture marked TM is taken from *The Message: The New Testament in Contemporary Language*. Colorado Springs: NavPress, 1993.

Scripture marked KJV is taken from the King James Version of the Bible.

To discover God in the smallest and most ordinary things, as well as in the greatest, is to possess a rare and sublime faith.

Souls who recognize God in the most trivial, the most grievous, and the most mortifying things that happen to them in their lives, honour everything equally with delight and rejoicing and welcome with open arms what others would dread and avoid.

Jean-Pierre de Caussade
The Sacrament of the Present Moment

Contents

PART 1: MY FIRST, FAINT AWARENESS 9

Watching God Work
Discovering God in the Great and the Ordinary 11

Lean on Me
A New Life Out of Solitude 21

The "Be" Ethic
God Looks on the Heart 28

Plumbing the Depths
The Recognition of Sin 37

Ron's Combo Gumbo
Finding God in the Family 46

What Do I Really Want to Do?
Knowing God's Will 54

PART 2: SPIRITUAL CULTURE SHOCK 61

What You See Is What You Get
Practicing the Art of Watching God Work 65

God Works on Bourbon St.
Finding God in the Dark 74

The View from the Piano Bench
Seeing God in Others' Lives 80

'Tis a Gift to Be Simple
The Undivided Heart 90

Finding God at the Bijou
"Whatever is pure . . . think about such things" 97

No Man Is an Island
Learning about the Body of Christ 103

Ordinary Sinners
God Works through Our Weakness 109

ADD with H
"Be still and know that I am God" 115

A Declaration of Dependence
God's Part in Our Growth 120

PART 3: THE LONG JOURNEY 127

To Live Is to Dance
Watching God Work through the Pain 129

Out of the Holy Huddle
Beyond Introspection 136

Grow Old Along with Me
Watching God Work in Old Age 142

My New Year's Resolution
The Humility I Haven't Achieved 148

The Problem of Not Understanding
God Works in Wondrous Ways 155

Four Things I Know for Sure
God Isn't Done with Me Yet 165

Do You Know What You've Got?
Beginning a Life of Watching God Work 175

EPILOGUE
My Secret Life as a Bibliophile 180

A LITTLE HELP FROM MY FRIENDS 187

PART 1

My First, Faint Awareness

Some spiritual truths I have grasped over the years with more intensity than others. One of those is that at any time God will give us grace to begin again. When we fall, he helps us up. Make a royal mess of our lives, and we can start fresh. It's become a cliché, but today is the first day of the rest of your life. No wonder the story of the Prodigal Son is so popular.

I have long been aware that a deeper spiritual life and a more intimate relationship with Christ is possible. In recent years, however, I have begun a bonding with God that has brought more satisfaction than I've ever known. And I have a strong desire to tell about it.

Unfortunately it took a traumatic loss in my life to beget the desperation necessary to stay the course of this journey. I write now after only several years of what is truly a new spiritual experience. I feel like a learner, and I have the enthusiasm of a new believer. I can't separate what I've learned from the mundane, daily events of my life, so I'll tell a few stories on myself, and I'll begin with my first, faint awareness that God had something special in store for me.

Watching God Work

Discovering God in the Great and the Ordinary

Our convention hosts had taken us to a dude ranch in Colorado Springs for a "banquet." Steak and beans on a tin plate, a little country music, a few speeches, and we'd close up another annual gathering of Christian editors. I met Roger as we entered the dining hall, and he suggested we sit together. I knew him only casually as the editor of *Decision* magazine. He was well-respected by our colleagues, a gentleman, sincere and personal, often with a hint of humor in his style.

Elbow to elbow we sat on backless benches at long, wooden tables, and Roger asked what was happening in my life. I had just become engaged to be married and was quick to tell anyone who gave me a chance. "That explains it," he replied. He had noticed me at the convention a year ago, one of the walking wounded, only four months after my wife, Carole, had died. But this year he felt I had a quicker step, a livelier spirit.

A few weeks later Roger wrote to ask if I would write an article on "Falling in Love—Again" for the February Valentine's issue of *Decision*. He wanted something that would help readers see God at work and help them understand his Word.

It was an easy assignment. In the previous few years I had gone through a painful passage of life in which I had urgently, often desperately, sought God. I had developed a fierce determination to know him as I had never known him before. I had curled up in a favorite corner and read, listened, and meditated for hours. I even had one special image and prayer—I asked God to wrap his arms around me and hold me.

I had been a Christian for more than forty years, since I was a freshman in college, and in my pilgrimage I had often stumbled and wandered. But I had always returned. Or I should say, God picked me up and set me back on the right road. Now in a period of two short years I had learned more about God and had drawn closer to him than at any time in my life.

Just as important, however, during this time I had developed a new awareness of God working in me and around me. Not that I ever believed that God takes time off. The Spirit works continually and tirelessly, I'm sure, to shape us in the image of Christ. I simply hadn't paid as much attention. I hadn't stopped as often to ask and to notice what he was doing. However, in that first year after Carole died, I had begun to distinguish the clear evidence of a loving God in common and casual events. So when I met Mary and we began to note our mutual attraction to each other, I chose to believe that God was in it, that it was providence—that is, his way of providing for both of us. I was reluctant to concede that God was simply a spectator to our courtship.

I had always been quick to see God at work in the major events of my life. When I was offered a job or a child was born or my wife acquired a terminal illness, I was prone to see God working in the situation. But then I began to see God working in the mundane as well—in a casual conversation at a conference, in the antics of a child, in an uncomfortable marital quarrel.

I don't mean to imply that God pulls the strings of our lives like a giant puppeteer. I don't believe he arranges circumstances to get his point across here or there. I simply mean he allows the circumstances to achieve his purpose—which is to draw his people to himself and complete the work he has begun in them.

Believing God, that is, receiving the truth of the gospel, is simply the first step into the Christian life. From then on by the power of his Spirit we must strive for perfection, and one way to do this is to seek him in every odd corner of our lives, as well as in the obvious. As *The Westminster Confession of Faith* puts it, "A continual and irreconcilable war rages in every believer." The old nature challenges the new, and while it delivers a few bruising punches and wins a few rounds, it is more and more subdued as we let the Spirit reign in our lives.

Watching God work means having a ringside seat at this battle. It means dancing at each victory and mourning over each defeat. It means cheering on the Spirit, to press the metaphor, and noting the tricks of the flesh, so we won't fall into the same trap again. It means seeing clearly the sanctifying work of the Spirit of Christ and rejoicing in our gradual growth toward holiness.

Most of the time we don't see the changes. We can't record the exact moment we overcame a bad habit, shifted our thinking, or became just a little more like Christ. But we know they happen. On a doorjamb in our kitchen we mark the growth spurts of our adolescent son. We can't actually see Clint grow, but the evidence is there in pencil, as well as in the too-tight jeans, shirts, and shoes he regularly discards. So it is in the spiritual life. If we pay attention, contemplate what's around us, and reflect on the Word, we can be more aware of God at work. We can see him pushing a little here, pulling a little there, always providing, always loving, always working.

Nor am I suggesting that I have a magic formula for finding God or a twelve-step program for knowing his will. It isn't always clear to me why God allows certain things to happen. While working on this manuscript, a friend loaned me the use of a lovely vacation home on a lake. So I packed my computer, a salesman's sample case full of books and files, and a box of food and drove two and a half hours to the lake. Pieces of the manuscript ran through my mind as I got closer to the lake. I was geared up, looking forward to the isolation, and ready to write, with nothing to interrupt me for three days. No phone, no television, no family or friends.

The last stretch before the home is a steep, rocky road, and as I drove down it, I noticed lights in the windows and smoke coming from the chimney. Puzzled, and with a sense of foreboding, I parked, rang the bell, then learned the worst. There had been a mixup. The co-owner of the house had loaned it to someone else who planned to be there for a few days.

Frustrated and deeply disappointed, I got back in my car, drove the two and a half hours home, unpacked the computer, food, books, and clothes and asked God what I was supposed to understand in this. The answer I received was "Trust me! You don't need to know why I do everything. I'm working in your life, and you won't understand it all. Just trust me."

This idea of watching God work is not new. In a wonderful little book called *The Sacrament of the Present Moment*, a French priest named Jean-Pierre de Caussade instructs us "to discover God in the smallest and most ordinary things, as well as in the greatest." To do this, he writes, "is to possess a rare and sublime faith." John Wesley warns that "it is a childish conceit to suppose chance governs the world . . . even in those things that appear to be casual."

In *Prayer: Finding the Heart's True Home*, Richard Foster writes, "God wants us to be present where we are. He invites us to see and to hear what is around us, and through it all, to discern the footprints of the Holy." And Catherine Marshall, in *Something More*, assures us that "nothing can happen to us without his knowledge, his consent, and his participating Presence as Saviour," that "no detail of any life is too insignificant for his loving providence."

Finally, we have Jesus' promise that even a sparrow cannot fall to the ground apart from the will of the Father and that the very hairs of our head are numbered.

In this book I've recorded some routine and seemingly commonplace incidents in my life, as well as some major events. The first months of my growing awareness of God at work were eventful times in which I gave up the single life, plunged into a blended family, and reentered fatherhood. I survived the first family vacation, explored the idea of adoption, and relearned a lot about submission. But this practice of watching for the hand of God working has grown in fits and starts, even as I returned to a more routine existence. It will in due time, I pray, become a fixed habit.

Some of these chapters rehearse happy or humorous times; others account for more poignant or sorrowful moments. Many of them uncover the pain that is a plentiful and essential ingredient in the process of becoming like Christ. But in each of the incidents I describe, God clearly revealed himself. And if I was paying attention, the revelation could result in my knowing him better and in bearing his image more faithfully.

I recognize a danger in relating my own personal experiences. I've tried to wrench off a corner of the mask I normally present to the world and let you see a little of me in the flesh, even when it's not a very pretty sight. But God has made changes for the better, and I've told those stories as well because they hold more hope and encouragement than does the rehearsing of my sins.

The last thing I want to do, however, is convey an attitude of "Hey, look at me! See how far I've come." James, the brother of Jesus, writes, "Anyone who sets himself up as 'religious' by talking a good game is self-deceived. This kind of religion is hot air and only hot air" (James 1:26 TM). To begin with, I don't understand why some forty years ago God chose to make himself known to me. But *he* did it. Nor do I completely understand why in recent years he has moved in my heart to respond the way I have. All I know, again, is that it wasn't something I suddenly decided to do. *He* initiated it.

To tell my story I've used theological terms such as salvation and sanctification. But this is not a book about doctrine. This is about experience. Doctrine is important, but it's not the same as experience. To press a metaphor used by C. S. Lewis in *Mere Christianity*, there is a difference between theories of nutrition and a good meal. "All sensible people know," Lewis writes, "that if you are tired and hungry a meal will do you good." But a man can eat his dinner, he goes on, "without understanding exactly how food nourishes him." Just so, there is a difference between an organized set of beliefs and Christianity. I write to tell you about the meal, not to explain why and how it has nourished me.

On top of that I relate these events because many of us find it hard to believe that our friends are truly like us. We assume we are different. We have temptations, hurts, fantasies, and ideas that no one else has or would understand. In fact, if we told them about some of our struggles and strange ideas, they'd keep their distance in the future. "How weird!" they'd say to themselves.

I incline that way at times, though I know in my heart it's not true. In reality I believe some will find solace or encouragement or strength or counsel in hearing my story and knowing they are not alone. What we suffer "we suffer in communion with all of humanity, yes, all of creation," Henri Nouwen writes in *The New Oxford Review*. "Healing begins with taking our pain out of its diabolic isolation." And recognizing the commonality of our joys and successes. The Christian life, it is often said, cannot be lived in isolation. Small pleasures and deep satisfactions, as well as doubts, failures, and temptations, find meaning in community.

So while others have set out the steps to know God better, I've chosen to tell what happened to me, in the hope that these accounts will help you detect the Creator at work in your life. I trust my reflections will inspire you to praise and thanksgiving. And I pray the stories will aid you in developing your own skills of observation, so his molding and shaping of your life might not be in vain.

God isn't done with me or you or with any of us. He who began a good work in us, Paul wrote to the Christians at Philippi, "will carry it on to completion until the day of Christ Jesus" (Phil. 1:6). There is movement in the Christian life. God has a goal—our perfection—and watching him work in us to help us reach that goal can add excitement to our sometimes mundane lives. Being aware of his hand in our lives should encourage us to continue, as Paul also urged the Philippians, "to work out [our] salvation with fear and trembling" (Phil. 2:12).

Lean on Me

A New Life Out of Solitude

I didn't want to go to Houston. I had no stomach for the affected gaiety of a convention or the bonhomie of colleagues who meant well but to whom I couldn't explain the gloom I wore like a secondhand suit.

"Hi, Fred!"

"Hi, Ron! How are you?"

Do you really want to know? I thought. *I'm down, way down, and I can't get up. My wife died and except for a few trusted friends, I don't want to talk about it. In fact, I don't even want to talk.*

But I had to talk. That's why I was there. I had promised to lead a workshop in, of all things, public relations.

The byword of these gatherings is "Hey, good to see you!" and I often wondered who really meant it. So when Russ Reid, who had asked me to lead the workshop, hailed me with "Hey, let's get together," I put him to the test. "Sure, Russ, when do you want to do it?"

Russ is a gregarious, hail-fellow type, and when he searched his schedule and couldn't find an open slot except for nine o'clock that night, I had even more doubts. But for reasons I couldn't explain, I wanted to talk to Russ, so with some reservations I appeared at his hotel room at the appointed time.

That evening Russ told me his own story. He had gone through a difficult divorce that he didn't want. In the process he had read a book that helped him, so he recommended it to me. I could see the similarity of divorce and death—a huge, wrenching loss—so I duly noted the name of the book and later picked up a copy.

The book, Henri Nouwen's *Reaching Out*, fell apart after several readings. I still have the pieces with paragraphs marked in yellow and notes in the margins and dried coffee and tears mixed together, smudged over the pages. Here's what it says:

> New life is born out of the pains of the old.
> The spiritual life does not allow bypasses.
>
> In the midst of our irking loneliness we can find the beginnings of a quiet solitude.

The pain I felt in grief was only to be expected, of course. Skip Ryan, my pastor, had told me it was as though a piece of me had been wrenched away, leaving a gaping hole. Of course it hurt. And it would take time to heal.

But I knew there was more to it than that. I knew something Skip didn't know. Over the long years of marriage I had made Carole my reason for being. She was my ground, my sustenance. When she was unhappy with me, I was miserable. When she pulled away into her own world, as she did at times, I felt completely alone. Of course I had let her down, probably more often than she had deserted me. Still I had put her first in my life. I had never truly learned that in the midst of my irking loneliness, God would always be there in the solitude, and I could find my reason for being and my peace in him.

I suspect that many couples fall into this trap, and many marriages break up over unrealistic expectations. It's normal for us to feel loss when our beloved isn't there, but to require another individual for your survival, Scott Peck says in *The Road Less Traveled*, is parasitic. To be unable to function without the love and support of another is a pathologic dependency. No one should have that kind of burden imposed on him. And while I wasn't so dependent on Carole's love that I absolutely couldn't function without her, I had allowed her favor to determine to a great extent the quality of my personal peace and happiness. So I needed more than just the healing of the wound caused by losing her. I needed to learn a new way of living. I needed to know God more intimately than I had ever known him before.

In my single state I realized I had no other choice but to lean on God. I had no one else. And I might remain single the rest of my life. I had no idea whether or not God had planned someone else for me. I knew I'd better learn, and learn fast, to lean solely on him.

So in the months ahead I spent hour after hour in solitude. I curled up in a favorite spot in my bedroom with a view of the woods and read and prayed. If I felt especially lonely, I asked God to wrap his arms around me, and I saw it in my mind—the arms of God holding me, comforting me, even rocking me as my mother and father had done. I wasn't abandoned. I wasn't alone. I had come in desperation because I had no place else to go, and slowly the healing began.

It was a beginning, a first, faint awareness of a new kind of living and the desire to reengage life and find God in it. This was living with an awareness of God around me. It was a breakdown of the old segmentation of sacred and secular moments of life.

In *Reaching Out* Henri Nouwen tells the story of the priest who canceled his subscription to the *New York Times* because the endless bad news disturbed him and kept him from God. It saddened Nouwen because it implied that we can find God only in an artificial retreat. Instead Nouwen argues that "a real spiritual life

. . . makes us so aware of the world around us, that all that is and happens becomes part of our contemplation and meditation and invites us to a fearless response." This, I believed, was slowly coming to pass in my life.

About ten months after the incident in Houston, I wrote to some friends that "if I had had a goal for the past year, it was, first, to get through the year. More than that, however, I wanted to learn to live in solitude and know that I could live alone with a peace that clearly comes from God." I had done that. God had given me that assurance. New life was rising from the pains of the old. I had lived those last months with both a sense of leaning on him alone and expecting him to work. And that's when I noticed Mary.

I had known her only slightly, a widow with three children still in school, a member of my church. So with more than just moderate curiosity about how God was working in this instance, I asked her out for dinner.

For our first date I chose a charming country inn with a homey, intimate, and romantic atmosphere. If you had asked me, I would have firmly denied I had romance in mind. I was, I told myself and others, simply looking for female companionship.

That evening, to my surprise, I found myself a little nervous. After all, why should I, with three grown children, a sensible, experienced-in-the-ways-of-the-world widower, feel like an adolescent on a first date?

Still, I wondered if the conversation would drag. Would I say something foolish? Spill soup on my tie?

The conversation, it turned out, didn't drag. In fact diners came and went while Mary and I lingered for four hours. By then I was no longer nervous; I was captivated.

Age may confer a degree of wisdom, but it suffers from a certain amount of forgetfulness, and in the next few months I rediscovered what I had long ago forgotten about love: Love inflates the ego. Partners endlessly exaggerate each other's virtues, caress their loved one with compliments, and ignore obvious character defects and shortcomings. Marriage most often cures this. In time, like an aircraft landing in a storm, marriage brings us on a bumpy ride back to earth where on wobbly legs we regain our equilibrium. But I was a long way from that. Besides I had ridden that rocket before, so I knew that love only temporarily repeals the law of gravity. I had once known those feelings of weightlessness and invincibility associated with falling in love, and they had led to a sound marriage in which my wife kept my feet firmly planted on earth. But that was years ago.

Love also fogs the brain, and I was determined that in my flighty condition, unbecoming my age, I would not forget the lesson I had just recently learned—of dependence on God alone. I knew it would be easy to slip into another relationship in which God took second place. When Mary and I decided to marry, we talked about this, and we chose Matthew 6:33 ("Seek first his kingdom and his righteousness, and all these things will be given to you as well") to inscribe inside our wedding bands. We wanted to inscribe in our hearts as well the idea that God, not our spouse, would provide all our needs.

A new chapter in my spiritual life heralded a new relationship of marriage. It was easy to find God in this auspicious beginning, but would I still see him in the ordinary and mundane things to come?

The "Be" Ethic

God Looks on the Heart

We were halfway up Doi Inthanon, the highest mountain in Thailand, when I asked Leona if she liked Willie Nelson. The old pickup truck we were in had a cassette player, and as she shifted up and down, negotiating the turns and the ruts and inching as far as possible away from the edge of the cliffs, I thought a little country music might help my nerves.

"Willie who?" Leona asked.

I glanced over to see if she was joking, but she wasn't.

Leona is a missionary who has spent thirty years, half of her life, in that part of the world teaching the tribal people about Jesus. She has returned to the States on occasion, whenever the mission required it, but she prefers the mountain villages where she often lives months at a time with the Hmong tribe. Willie Nelson, whose gravelly tones I find soothing, might be a clerk at a 7-Eleven for all she knew. Except that 7-Eleven didn't ring a bell with Leona either.

I ran a little name recognition test on Leona that morning. When I asked her about Tom Brokaw, Nintendo, and frozen yogurt, she smiled and shook her head. Domino's doesn't deliver in Leona's neighborhood, nor have many of the newer accoutrements of our culture shown up in those hills. But Leona had found a life there. She had often trekked ten or twelve hours at a time where no vehicle could pass. She had faced ambush by Communist guerrillas, endured sickness, loneliness, resistance, and rejection because, as she put it, "most of the people in the mountains have never heard about Jesus." I was so impressed that later I wrote a story about Leona and called it, "Goodbye, Willie Nelson; Hello, Big Mountain."

Several months later as I celebrated my sixtieth birthday, I thought about Leona. We were the same age and cut from the same generational and cultural cloth. We were the post–World War II crowd. Historians say we sought prosperity and conformity. We didn't protest or ask questions as we meekly marched off to war (Korea) or the mission field.

Typical of the age, I developed a strong work ethic and often prayed, "Lord, use me." I was inspired by hymns such as "Work for the Night Is Coming" and words such as these by Charles Wesley:

> To serve the present age,
> My calling to fulfill;

O may it all my powers engage,
To do my Master's will.

I suspect that Leona and many of our generation did the same. The author Frederick Buechner, only a few years our senior, wrote of the same urge. He was a young man in the early 1950s when he discovered "the possibility, at least, of a life in Christ, with Christ, and, on some fine day conceivably, even a life for Christ," as he put it in *Now and Then.* And later he added, "*I wanted to do something for him.*" (The italics for emphasis are his.)

I discovered writing in the '50s. I found great satisfaction and a degree of success in it and became convinced the Lord had granted me both the satisfaction and the success to point me to my vocation. I grew to believe he wanted me to use these gifts for him. The old New England family of which I was a part had a well-developed, Puritan work ethic, and a primary guiding principle in my life has been to find the place God could use me.

Forty years later, however, I have come to believe I need a "*be*" ethic more than I need a *work* ethic. On the shady side of sixty I see that God is more interested in who I am than what I do. While I set goals and measure success in numbers, God says, "Sit still and listen." While I emphasize performance and accomplishment, God looks for the fruit of the Spirit: love, joy, peace, patience, kindness, goodness, faithfulness, gentleness, and self-control. While I love the songs about service, he whispers, "Blessed are the poor in spirit and those who hunger and thirst after righteousness."

The whole weight of the Scripture points to this truth. Noah *walked* with God. Abraham *believed* God, and God gave him credit for his faith. David, Acts 13:22 says, was a man after God's own heart. Peter, the apostle who had to be doing something all the time, confessed, "You are the Christ," and this simple confession of faith brought the Lord's blessing on him. God blessed them not for what they had done, not because they served him or did anything for him, but because of their belief in him.

Alas, today we are as awash in the busyness of service as any generation ever has been. Committee meetings, projects, programs, and events distract us and leave little time to "be still, and know that I am God" (Ps. 46:10). When service becomes our priority, we quickly fill our calendars. When it's more important for us to *do* something (whether it's for God or for someone else), we have little time left to listen and watch and see God at work around us. I once heard of some guidance counselors who asked students to write their obituary and include in it what they had accomplished. I'd take a different approach. I'd have them write what they want to become. Describe the person they want to be.

All this is not to belittle service. It is only to put it in its place. Good works follow faith. Doing springs from being. As we're changed into his likeness from the inside, we'll respond to human needs on the outside. I still struggle with the desire to do something in the name of Christ that will make a difference in this world. And I realize much of this springs from a desire to earn God's favor, to get points in God's scorebook, to expunge the old or at least build up the credit side of my heavenly ledger. Service that blossoms purely from the love of God glorifies God. But service that springs from a desire to earn the favor of God or man is worth nothing in the sight of God.

The chief end of man, the catechism says, is not to serve God and accomplish great things for him; it is to glorify him, to become like him, to bask in the blessing of his smile as we reflect his goodness. My self-worth comes from being his son, his beloved creation, and he measures the degree to which I become like him, to which I reflect his likeness, not what I produce.

I don't know whether it's harder to do this in our society than it has been in others. We certainly find some tension between our need to measure time and accomplishment and our desire to become like Christ. We live by the clock and by the schedule, and we measure it all by what we produce—how many widgets we stamp out, patients we examine, policies we sell, new members we bring in. We not only build our bank accounts with the results of our work, we gauge our self-worth by it as well. I produce; therefore I am. (The other side of the coin of production is consumption. The society that values those who produce goods must also value those who consume them. I shop; therefore I am.)

In defense of this generation I'll admit that we have more today to distract us from focusing on our internal state. Television, observes Ken Myers, "is much better at displaying external realities than leading us to consider the complexities of internal realities. It thus tends to prejudice viewers in favor of movement over contemplation, becoming over being." But the "good life," Myers adds, "is really more being than doing."

Technology also seduces us. The owner of a public relations firm writes that she "became one of the last people in America to acquire a portable radio/headphone set." Why? Because "once I was fully plugged in, things stopped occurring to me." Her success depended on ideas, and she needed quiet time, so to speak, to hear the voice of creativity. "If Newton had been wearing his Walkman," she added, "he probably would have overlooked the real impact of the apple's fall."

I suspect, however, that my ancestors who cleared the woods and farmed the black soil just west of

Boston some 300 years ago had no more discretionary time than I do today. Life was simpler but life was harder, and the basic functions took more time. Technology has not only given us comfort and convenience but increased the leisure time available to us to stop and think about who we are.

Avoiding serious thought about the meaning of life by staying busy is as old, perhaps, as Adam. We fill our calendars because we want to. "When we have no project to finish," Henri Nouwen writes in *Reaching Out*, "no friend to visit, no book to read, no television to watch or no record to play, and when we are left all alone by ourselves we are brought so close to the revelation of our basic human aloneness and are so afraid of experiencing an all-pervasive sense of loneliness that we will do anything to get busy again and continue the game which makes us believe that everything is fine." Avoiding God is also another variation on the ultimate rebellion of putting ourselves in the place of God.

I came to understand the need for an "ethic of being" not through any wisdom bestowed by age but by the necessity of the circumstances thrust upon me. I came lately to welcome, even long for, the stillness in which I know that he is God. And it is in that stillness that he blends all the circumstances and produces something new. As I said, the onset of my sixth decade triggered some of these reflections. When my productive days are over—and they're decidedly not—I'll still have plenty of room for becoming, for letting God continue his work of making me in his image, but I can't wait till then.

The last I heard, Leona still makes regular trips up into the mountains, negotiating the rutted roads and ministering to her beloved Hmong, and I suspect she'll do that as long as she has strength. I also suspect she has learned, probably long before I did, that while God accepts her service, he is more interested in her heart. Somewhere in the clear mountain air she finds time, I'm sure, to sit still and listen for the voice of God, to put being before doing.

For me in recent years the habit of watching God work and the attempt to find him in ordinary events and in each moment of the day has served as a buffer against the pressure of production. It has helped to sound the alarm when I begin to see my value in how much I do.

At about age ten I learned what my Sunday school teacher called the Be-Attitudes. They were just that—attitudes, qualities, states of being. And they were at the heart of the teachings of Jesus. A paraphrase of the fourth one reads: "O the bliss of the man who longs for total righteousness as a starving man longs for food, and as a man perishing of thirst longs for water." And then Jesus added, "For that man will be truly satisfied."

There is one caveat to all of this, however. The more time we spend in the company of a holy God, the more we're conscious of the mess that threatens to burst out of the closet of our lives. And it's not a pretty sight.

Plumbing the Depths

The Recognition of Sin

As a boy I learned a ditty from my mother and sang it gleefully. It went:

Nobody loves me.
Everybody hates me.
I'm going to the garden to eat worms.
Big, fat, juicy ones,
Slippery, slimy, wiggly ones,
Fuzzy wuzzy, dirty, wooly worms.

Given the current popularity of a good sense of self-worth, no enlightened mother would sing that to her child today. My mother sang it to me when I moped around feeling sorry for myself, but it provoked a disturbing thought that I never told her: *If people knew how bad I really was, they wouldn't love me, so I deserved to go to the garden to eat worms.*

Sad notion for a boy to harbor; nevertheless there is a bit of biblical truth here that we would do well to come to grips with. The truth is this: Few of us could bear for any length of time the sight of our sin as God sees it. J. I. Packer expressed it well: "In moral and spiritual terms, we are all sick and damaged, diseased and deformed, scarred and sore, lame and lopsided, to a far, far greater extent than we realize."

I heard about an eight-year-old boy who lied to his dad about a prank he played. As part of a gang he threw a dead rat on the porch of a crotchety old man, and when the man called the boy's father to complain, the boy denied it. Promptly after that, however, the boy went out to the garage and scratched on the wall, "I get blamed for things I didn't do." The truth was so difficult to live with, he changed it. His sin was too much for him to admit, so he denied it, even to himself.

When we spend a lot of time with God and watching God work in our lives and in the world around us, we begin to sense his holiness, and this in turn makes us conscious of our unholiness. The better we know God, the more we are aware of the depth and deceitfulness of our sin (that is, the amazing ability we have to rationalize and deny that sin is sin), and this produces sanctifying results.

For example, I've never been a world-class submitter. My pride runs deep, and I've often caught myself on the verge of muttering, "I have a right to . . ." before I decide to give up whatever rights I imagine I have. But occasionally I catch a glimpse of how driven I am to get what I want. I recognize the self-serving motives that have been covered over with layer after layer of rationalization, and I'm moved by the need for submission. In true submission, says Richard Foster in *Celebration of Discipline*, we finally "lay down the terrible burden of always needing to get our own way."

True submission says I give up the right to do what I want for the sake of someone else. It's motivated by love and respect, not forced by law or outside pressure. It acts with eyes open, knowing why it lays down its rights. It's a rare quality, and it takes practice.

Mary had been single for five years before we met, and as the only adult in the household, she called the shots for three kids, two dogs, two cats, and a hamster. She decided what they were going to eat and when. She set the thermostat, chose the church, coped with schools, planned the vacations, and arranged the furniture—all by herself.

I had lived alone for a year and a half. I had told myself during that time that I didn't choose to be single, but if that's the way God wanted it, I was going to enjoy it. I lived in a big house. I arranged the furniture, set the thermostat, invited whom I wanted to dinner, and came and went without telling a soul. I balanced my own checkbook (at least I tried), bought what I wanted to eat, went on vacation by myself, and called it a day and went to bed whenever I pleased.

Then we got married.

We knew that marriage requires mutual submission. We had both tried to practice it in a former marriage, but now we wondered if our temporary freedom had gone to our heads. How would we handle the sobriety of sharing decisions as well as space?

Well, we've been tripped up by how to arrange the glasses in the dishwasher, which route to take driving downtown, and what our ninth grader takes for lunch. On occasion we've raised our voices a frequency or two in discussing national politics, the local school system, or the imminent moral collapse of our society, but these have added more color to the day than tension to the atmosphere, and in these more weighty areas we seem to know when to back off. We feel more intensely, however, about the height of the grass when company is coming or whether we buy 2 percent, 1 percent, or skim milk.

Submission in marriage is a much-maligned doctrine. The church today has often been hung up on who is the head and overlooked the idea of "one another" (Eph. 5:21). In marriage we blend diverse personalities with dissimilar gifts, bents, and opinions, but with equal rights—and equal obligation to submit. But if I read the Scriptures correctly, I submit to Mary, not because she's right—and she often is where I am wrong—nor because of some grand idea of unselfishness, nor because of my love for her. I choose to yield my will to hers out of love and reverence for Jesus Christ who made her in his image and who submitted so much more for me.

Submission, in all areas of life, not just marriage, has come slowly for me, but the example of Christ's submission, as Paul described it to the Philippians, has greatly stimulated the process. "Your attitude should be the same as that of Christ Jesus," Paul writes, "who, being in very nature God, did not consider equality with God something to be grasped, but made himself nothing, taking the very nature of a servant, being made in human likeness. And being found in appearance as a man, he humbled himself and became obedient to death—even death on a cross" (Phil. 2:5–8). It is less difficult for me to submit to those I think are better, smarter, and wiser, although I often struggle even with that. But at times I've been called to submit to those for whom I have little respect—someone for whom I work, a civil authority, the director of an organization—and contemplating the truths above makes it much easier to do that.

This recognition of our sin that is brought on by spending time with a holy God should also bring a measure of transparency to our lives. This is the quality the psalmist described as "an undivided heart." It's a heart and mind so focused on pleasing God that all secondary, self-serving motives are squeezed out.

In *The Hiding Place*, Corrie ten Boom tells a delightful story about her father. In the pre–World War II city of Haarlem, the old Dutch watchmaker had a competitor, a Mr. Kan, who occasionally came to call on the ten Booms. "Father treated Mr. Kan's frequent visits," Corrie recalls, "as social calls from a cherished friend. 'Can't you see what he's doing?' I would rage after Mr. Kan had gone. 'He's finding out how much we're charging so he can undersell us!' Mr. Kan's display window always featured in bold figures prices exactly five guilders below our own.

"And Father's face would light up with a kind of pleased surprise as it always did on those rare occasions when he thought about the business side of watchmaking. 'But Corrie, people will save money when they buy from him!' And then he would always add, 'I wonder how he does it?'"

I find an appealing lack of guile in the old man's response. If he did understand what the other watchmaker was doing, he apparently wasn't troubled too much by it. But I think he truly had difficulty grasping the devious nature of the man's visits. He had no idea that the world looks down on such innocence as his. His hung out, and it annoyed his more down-to-earth daughter.

This combination of openness and honesty is a quality I both covet and fear. Two of my best friends have a great degree of it. You look at these men, and you can read them. They flash the emotion of the moment—anger, delight, pessimism, enthusiasm, disappointment—like a neon sign. They don't try to impress. A pastor once told me that he liked one of these men because the man didn't have "an agenda." Both men appear to have a childlike inability to cover up their motivations and their true feelings. No surprises! What you see is what you get! And both men have a deep sense of their own sin.

Sometimes I feel my two friends are caught off guard by the duplicity of people around them. They're not so naive that they're completely surprised by manipulation and deceit, but with their transparency comes a certain expectation that everyone else is the same way. And, to their credit, they're easily wounded.

I think this is the biblical ideal. It's what Jesus was talking about when he said if we seek first the kingdom of God, all these things will be given to us. Seek to please me and love Mr. Kan, the Lord told Mr. ten Boom, and don't worry about your watch business or your competitors, and I'll take care of you.

I'd love to exhibit that virtue, but when I examine my heart carefully, I find I have a secondary agenda. I cling to a cache of manipulative intentions that aren't pretty. The Spirit is working in me to point them out, but I have trouble letting go of them. That's partly a lack of trust in the Lord, I know. I fear the world will laugh at me. Transparent people have a hard time in life because the world rejects and mocks that quality.

Dostoyevsky imbued Prince Myshkin, the central figure in *The Idiot*, with a naivete that was rarely appreciated. On a train approaching St. Petersburg, Myshkin was drawn into conversation with a worldly wise and somewhat cynical man. The readiness of Myshkin, Dostoyevsky writes, "to answer all his companion's inquiries was remarkable. He betrayed no suspicion of the extreme impertinence of some of his [the companion's] misplaced and idle questions." His honesty was then scorned by the man, who told him that he was "straightforward and simplehearted" and "a regular blessed innocent and God loves such as you."

Myshkin is considered a type of Christ. And while I long for such a simple, Christ-like spirit, I don't want people to think I'm an idiot or a fool. The risk in revealing myself is rejection, by both the world and those close to me. I can do a passable job of handling rejection by the world, but it's much more difficult with those I love. The Father ten Booms and Prince Myshkins, while sometimes held in uncertain respect, are more often misunderstood, scorned, and trampled on, and that takes a lot of grace to handle.

The biblical command to be perfect is not impossible. It's not, as C. S. Lewis writes in *Mere Christianity*, "an idealistic gas. . . . If we let Him—for we can prevent Him if we choose—He will make the feeblest and filthiest of us into a god or goddess, a dazzling, radiant, immortal creature, pulsating all through with such energy and joy and wisdom and love as we cannot now imagine, a bright stainless mirror which reflects back to God perfectly (though, of course, on a smaller scale) His own boundless power and delight and goodness. The process will be long and in parts very painful; but that is what we are in for. Nothing less."

The more we sharpen our skills of God-watching, the more uncomfortable we'll be with our sins. Peter, confronted with Jesus for the first time, fell on his knees, in spite of the fact that his boat was about to sink, and cried, "Go away from me, Lord; I am a sinful man" (Luke 5:8). When Isaiah saw the Lord in a vision, he cried, "I am ruined. For I am a man of unclean lips" (Isa. 6:15). And he expected to die. Paul was struck blind when he encountered Jesus on the road to Damascus. The contrast between God's holiness and our unholiness is so great, we're physically affected when it becomes apparent to us.

The good news in all this, of course, is that we don't have to look at our sin very long. I don't mean we can cop out with a little cheap grace—"Hey, I don't have to worry; Christ died for me!" But the very submission of Christ I've been talking about has made possible the forgiveness of all my sins, which God has promised to put behind him as far as Omaha is from Hong Kong. Even farther!

Ron's Combo Gumbo

Finding God in the Family

I'm developing a small reputation, mostly through self-promotion, as a maker of a tasty Louisiana gumbo. Several years ago I combined a number of recipes, made a few adjustments of my own, and called it Ron's Combo Gumbo.

Making a pot of gumbo is a long (at least half a day) process that can't be hurried. You don't whip it up after work as a quick meal. I begin by cooking a chicken and pulling all the meat off the bones. Then I cook a pound or two of shrimp, remove the shells, and boil the shells in the water in which I cooked the shrimp. Later on, the stock from the shrimp and the chicken become part of the gumbo.

I make a roux from oil, butter, and flour and stir it for at least a half hour to get the right color. Some gumbo cooks insist the roux is the key to a good gumbo. By that point I've already chopped a half dozen or more vegetables, and I brown them in the roux. Then I add the stock and the seasonings for a long period of simmering. The chicken and sausage go in next, and the shrimp later. By this time the aroma fills the kitchen, and I add a dash of file powder to complete a pot of scrumptious, tangy Cajun gumbo.

I've come to believe gumbo is an almost perfect metaphor for a blended family. In fact the word is often used today as a synonym for *mixture*. While the ingredients are simmered together in one pot for a long time, and the entire concoction has a distinct flavor, you can easily pick out many of the ingredients that have retained a bit of their original personalities. Unlike Jell-O, for example, which combines ingredients, pours them into a mold, and comes out with one flavor, a good gumbo has many tastes.

The similarities to a blended family are obvious. The members come to the mix with already developed shapes and tastes and personalities that they don't easily lose. But the more they are simmered together, the more each takes on some of the whole. I don't need to press the metaphor to make the point here, but I think gumbo is a much more interesting culinary experience than Jell-O.

Frankly, it surprised me that God stuck me in the gumbo. As a widower living alone for months in a big house in the woods, I began to realize not only that I could live alone but that I could like it. The circumstances impose a kind of selfishness on those who live alone. You live much of your life without having to consider the needs of others. You can live sloppy or neat, eat well or warm up a can of soup. No one cares if you stay out all night or leave the lights burning or turn up the volume on the sound system.

But I also began to believe that if I wanted to know and serve God, I had more time to do it living alone. Without the responsibility of a family or the need to share my life with a wife and children, I had more time to devote to church or community service, to say nothing of the possibility of solitude. I often curled up with a book or spent time in meditation with only a rare interruption or demand. Suddenly I was dropped back into the simmering stew of a family, and this time it was a gumbo.

Do you truly desire to know God and find him in the ordinary and mundane things of life? There's no better place than in the midst of a family. How do we respond to the moods and insensitivities of those we know and love best? There our guard is down. How do we handle the minuscule provocations and minor domestic crises that come to every family? These reveal our true character. "Even when he was busiest in the kitchen," it was said about Brother Lawrence, the seventeenth century monk, "it was evident that the brother's spirit was dwelling in God. He often did the work that two usually did, but he was never seen to bustle. Rather, he gave each chore the time that it required, always preserving his modest and tranquil air, working neither slowly nor swiftly, dwelling in calmness of soul and unalterable peace." Try that sometime in the kitchen at about six in the evening with five people circling the room, one trying to cook, another setting the table, two who have just come home relating the events of the day, and the fifth one just wandering around getting in the way. "Brother Lawrence," his biographer commented, "saw nothing but the plan of God in everything" that happened to him.

Over the centuries, many have gone off into the desert to get closer to God, and some achieved the peace and sense of purpose they sought. "His soul being free of confusion, he held his outer senses also undisturbed," it was written about Antony, the first of the desert fathers. "So that from the soul's joy his face was cheerful as well, and from the movements of the body it was possible to sense and perceive the stable condition of the soul." It is, no doubt, easier to be single-minded and to focus on the Almighty without the distractions that others bring to our lives. But as de Caussade writes, "Souls who recognize God in the most trivial, the most grievous, and the most mortifying things that happen to them in their lives, honour everything equally with delight and rejoicing and welcome with open arms what others would dread and avoid" *(Sacrament)*. If God wanted me in the gumbo, well, he's the Cook.

The first hint I had that God was cooking up something came when I called on Mary for our second date. We had chosen a small Mexican restaurant for dinner, and as I waited for her to get ready, I made small talk with the children, and I imagined I was an object of curiosity. *Hmn! Who is this taking Mother out two weeks in a row?* As we left the house and walked toward the car, Mary commented casually, "Watch out, Ron, Clint is looking for a dad." Clint was nine at the time.

I gave the remark little thought that night, but it stuck in some recess of my mind, and I had occasion to ponder it later. When we began serious talk about a long-term relationship, Mary brought up the topic, and this time I couldn't dismiss it. Was I ready to father an adolescent again? Wasn't I a little old for that? Could I cope with Little League, wrestling on the living room rug, repairing bicycles? Could I live up to the expectations of a boy embarking on puberty?

To be truthful, I couldn't actually picture myself, at what I termed "advanced middle-age," going to parent-teacher meetings or teaching a boy to tie a necktie or watching reruns of "Ernest Goes to Jail." Clint was certainly likable, gregarious, and well-behaved, and, as far as I could tell, generally well-adjusted, but it was Mary I had fallen in love with and wanted to marry. I just had no strong feeling that I should return to fatherhood, but if this was God's idea for me, I felt sure he'd prepare me for the task, even though it was far from my mind at the moment.

I won't mislead you. It hasn't been one long pizza party. For example, I have only reluctantly acknowledged that the gospels say nothing about eating all your vegetables. And entering fully into the endless round of school and community activities common to the life of a middle-class suburban family has come slowly for me.

Still, I believe a bond has begun to form between Clint and me. I once thought bonding was something that happened between two pieces of wood or plastic when you applied contact cement. They may not stick in minutes, but give them overnight to dry, and you'll never pull them apart. The bonding of two lives, however, takes much more time.

Talk about bonding. For three Sunday mornings in a row, early into our new family experience, I stood behind Clint as we faced the mirror and tied his tie together. On the fourth Sunday he came to me, tie already tied and properly arranged under a bright and shining smile of satisfaction.

Occasionally during our first year of marriage Mary wished aloud that we had a history together, memories to recall. Now we have a few. We can look back, for example, and remember the Sunday morning we got up early to take the train to Washington. Clint had never ridden a train, and he was excited. But when we arrived at the station, we learned the train was four hours late. The day might have been a disaster, but we went out for a pancake breakfast, came home, read the Sunday comics while we waited, and finally went back to the station for a memorable, if somewhat abbreviated, outing.

In this family life, however, Mary more than anyone else has helped me find God in the commonplace and see him patiently working in my life. She has often put her finger on a sore spot of my life that needs healing. And while I've sometimes responded with a vehement defense of my behavior, I have on more than one occasion realized she was God's answer to my desire to know him better.

I confess to more than occasional doubt, discouragement, and frustration, but I know this marriage was God's idea. Blending our families is part of his plan. Prayer has had a lot to do with whatever successes our family gumbo has achieved. It's akin perhaps to the stirring of the roux, which must go on constantly. And to push the metaphor even further, grace is the final dash of file powder that thickens the blend and makes it a true gumbo.

I don't want to press this gumbo metaphor too hard, however. A gumbo is a thick, almost mysterious, soup.

Each person's gumbo is a little different, and with each spoonful you wonder *what's in this one?* Life can be like that. But I've found, on the other hand, there may be a certainty and a simplicity to a life lived in the presence of God.

What Do I Really Want to Do?

Knowing God's Will

> Delight yourself in the Lord
> and he will give you the desires
> of your heart.
>
> *Psalm 37:4*

In my junior year of college I helped a friend in his campaign for editor of the college newspaper. He won, and as a political plum I claimed the jobs of assistant editor and columnist. I loved it. I immersed myself in it, took a summer course in journalism, got high on rubber cement and printer's ink—figuratively of course—and went on the next year to take over his job as editor. I discovered then that I loved to write, edit, and arrange the pieces of a publication more than I loved most things in this world. What's more, I had some small talent for it.

So as I approached my college graduation and the critical, decision-making time, I began to think about a career in journalism. I had also discovered about that time that I was not equipped for what I had thought I was called to do. Most of my friends were planning to be pastors. They would be called to a church, stand in the pulpit, preach the Word, counsel the people, lead them as the undershepherd of the flock, and I knew that wasn't for me. For one thing I couldn't preach for sour apples. When I stood before a group, my legs turned into Jell-O, my mind to mush, and my mouth to dust. I began to see quite clearly I was called to some other kind of work. Could it be that my ministry would be behind a typewriter, not a pulpit?

As I thought about it, I put a small twist on a familiar verse from the Psalms that was a favorite for many college students. "Delight yourself in the Lord and he will give you the desires of your heart," went the verse, and the standard interpretation went something like this: If we make God the focus of our lives and find our pleasure in him, he will give us what we desire because we will want what he wants for us. But I began to believe that my love of writing and editing had been placed in my heart and mind by God because that's what he wanted me to do for him. It wasn't so much my discovering what God wanted as it was his placing the very desires themselves and the joy in the work into my heart. A small distinction, perhaps, but an important one for me at the time.

I've applied this principle over the years in the major decisions of my life. If I make God the focus of my life, I can be sure I'll know his will. I can ask, *What is it I really want?* believing that the Spirit of God will place those desires there. This woman I want to marry, this house I plan to buy, this job offered to me—if I am finding my daily delight in God, I can be assured my desires for these have come from God. Suddenly the old question about how to find God's will for my life is answered.

The conditional clause here, of course, is "Delight yourself in the Lord." Too often when I come into the presence of God, I have something in mind, some purpose I've devised. I seek forgiveness or guidance or blessing. Or I may have purposed to spend the time thanking or praising him. These are all pleasing to God, I'm sure. But I believe he also wants us to come without any plan, without any requests or awareness of needs, and spend time in fellowship with him. He wants us to enjoy his company, just as we come together with friends and find that being in their presence is a delight.

Recently I've begun to wonder if, as we do this, God will also reveal his will to us in the ordinary and mundane things of life, like choosing what foods we eat or deciding what books we read or games we play. "Nothing is more reasonable, perfect or divine," de Caussade writes in *Sacrament*, "than the will of God . . . and if you have been granted the secret of how to discover it in every moment, you have found what is most precious and desirable." If we abandon all restraint, carry our wishes to their furthest limits, open our hearts boundlessly, he goes on, "there is not a single moment when you will not be shown everything you can possibly wish for. The present moment holds infinite riches beyond your wildest dreams. . . ."

It is a comforting thought: I can know God's perfect will for me at every moment. Richard Foster develops this idea of perpetual communion with God in his book *Prayer*. In a chapter entitled "Unceasing Prayer," he cites a number of saints who have worked at what Brother Lawrence called "practicing the presence of God." "The time of business does not with me differ from the time of prayer," Lawrence wrote. "And in the noise and clatter of my kitchen, while several persons at the same time are calling for different things, I possess God in as great tranquility as if I were on my knees at the blessed sacrament."

The late Quaker Thomas Kelly, in his *Testament of Devotion*, claims that we can live on two mental levels. "On one level we may be thinking, discussing, seeing, calculating, meeting all the demands of external affairs. But deep within, at a profounder level, we may also be in prayer and adoration, song and worship and a gentle receptiveness to divine breathings."

While it is a startling idea, it makes more sense to me than the compartmentalizing of faith and daily affairs that I most often practice. If I meet with God in the morning, must I bid him, "Have a nice day!" as I do my wife or son, as though one of us were leaving? Must I divide the day into "God times" and other times? And if so, how much is God time and how much is other time? Is it not possible, as Brother Lawrence and Thomas Kelly have intimated, to maintain touch with God while doing all we do each day?

On a very practical level I have questioned whether there are things in life that require so much concentration, it's impossible to think of God while doing them. Driving on an icy road, for example. Or playing championship tennis. Studying for or taking a tough exam. While in graduate school I worked in a dairy doing simple bookkeeping. I had to check the daily sales sheets of each milkman to see that they balanced, then post those figures on another ledger. Each week I balanced that ledger and then posted the weekly total on a monthly sheet. That first semester I listened to the World Series with part of my mind while I did the bookkeeping with the other. And at the end of the month when I tried to balance it all, I learned the difficulty of trying to do two things at once. Still, Foster says, it is "arduous, yes, but not impossible."

Well, if it's true I can find God in all things and know his perfect will in every moment, then it only remains for me to believe it and obey. But there's the rub. It is unbelief that compartmentalizes. It is our unwillingness to trust that erects a wall between the God-life and the self-life. Stop believing, and we depart from his presence. Refuse to trust, and we say in effect, "Have a nice day, Lord. See you later." I know it only too well.

So I've chosen to take the first small step on the path toward discovering God's will throughout the day. I hesitate to talk about constant or perpetual communion with God as some of the saints have called it. I see it more as awareness.

Still, it takes discipline. I have to work at it, develop the habit. And while I have begun in a small way to acknowledge that presence more often throughout the day than I ever have before, still I go long periods as though I am on my own until some event or thought brings God back to mind.

Of course all this awareness means little without obedience. Mary, for example, desires and enjoys my verbal expressions of love and admiration. I may say, "I love you!" and point out her sensitivity to those in need or her skill as a mother, her willingness to please me or simply her beauty. But it wears thin if I simply mouth the words and neglect her wishes. Unless these expressions of my love are accompanied by attention to her needs and desires, they are empty.

Likewise with the Almighty. Faith leads to obedience, which is the evidence of love. I've sung the chorus "Trust and obey, for there's no other way," until that couplet seems almost trite. Yet the truth of it is fundamental to Christian faith. I could spend twenty-four hours a day in God's presence, but if I don't obey what I know to be his will, I must seriously doubt that I really believe.

Of course finding God's will does not necessarily mean understanding God's will. We have to contend with the eraser factor. We make mistakes. Not only is God's greater plan far beyond our ability to grasp, but pride, selfishness, slothfulness, lust, cloud our attempts to see the small part of it he has for us.

Nor does daily delighting ourselves in God automatically dispel all doubts. I find it interesting that it has not been in times of difficulty that I have wondered if Christianity is all an elaborate fantasy. In those times God has given me what Paul describes so beautifully and profoundly in his letter to the church at Rome: I have had strong confidence that absolutely nothing in heaven nor on earth could separate me from the love of God that I found in Jesus Christ. Instead it was when life was proceeding uneventfully that doubt, like the proverbial camel, stuck its nose into the tent of my life.

What is it I really want to do? God knows, and when he's ready, he will let me know. My assignment today is to delight myself in him. Looking back, however, I can readily remember a few times he changed my mind when I least expected it.

PART 2

Spiritual Culture Shock

The first time I left the confines of the continental United States I was shocked. I knew enough to expect unfamiliar ways and curious patterns of life. But that knowledge didn't necessarily help in coping with them when they came.

I had flown to Maracaibo, Venezuela, from Miami, Florida, to visit the printer who would print a publication I was helping to launch. I expected missionaries to meet me at the airport, but communication had broken down. I knew no one and hardly a word of Spanish. It was getting dark, and I had limited funds. The intense heat, the presence of armed guards around the terminal, the absence of street lights, and the strangeness of it all fed my growing anxiety.

Hours later after asking a stranger for help, I arrived at the mission compound and was shown to a flimsy board building with a corrugated metal roof and a narrow bunk in one room. I was to stay there that night, so I peeled off my damp clothes and sought the shower, only to encounter an even more shocking experience. As I turned on the light in the shower room, hundreds of cockroaches scurried around and over my feet, seeking a hole or a crack in which to hide. I had nowhere to hide, so, stark naked, I shrieked and began to dance around trying to avoid crushing the little critters with my bare feet. I can laugh now, and I refer to it as the time I learned the cockroach dance. But that first shock as I crossed a cultural border was a painful and emotionally draining experience.

Crossing spiritual frontiers can be like that. Like good missionaries we know that God has many of them for us and that we will learn from them. We desire them, not because of masochistic tendencies but because we know they draw us closer to him.

A few months into my new marriage, and into this new phase of my spiritual life, I had crossed more spiritual frontiers than I had for many years. I had learned that God was fashioning something from my pain. I discovered that many strata of sin lay buried far below the pleasant exterior landscape of my life. God had used my immersion in family life to expose me to new frontiers, and time and time again had revealed to me the sacrament of each present moment.

To use another metaphor, the road now began to take some unexpected turns. Nothing drastic. More often a pleasant surprise lay around a bend, or a break in the routine scenery revealed a spectacular vista of God's grace. Sometimes what appeared to be a dead end led to a glimpse of heaven, or an occasional patch of narrow, rough road smoothed out. Or a blind corner opened up just in time.

For example, I began to appreciate the need for discipline if I expected to see God at work. I have to pay attention. I uncovered a lack of concern for and interest in others that deeply disturbed me. And I was about to learn some practical lessons about the effect of my life, for good or bad, on the lives of others.

God loves to surprise us. It's characteristic of him, like a father who brings home something special for his children. We shout, "Whoopee!" and he adds an affectionate hug. And soon we begin to live with an eye toward heaven. What's next? What's God up to now?

As I've watched God work, I've come to expect the unusual and know that he is in it. As I've paid attention and listened, I've discovered him in the ordinary as well as in the wondrous. I haven't always understood the meaning, as the following stories make clear. But the trip has been anything but boring.

What You See Is What You Get

Practicing the Art of Watching God Work

Journalism teachers have a favorite exercise to spring on unsuspecting beginners. They arrange for several people to break into a class in the middle of a lecture or discussion and perform a mock crime such as an assault or a theft.

"Now," says the teacher after the intruders have left. "You are a reporter. Write down everything you saw and heard."

Journalists supposedly are trained to observe, to notice the color and style of a woman's dress, the mannerisms of a politician, the make and year of an automobile, the conversations and sounds around them. Accuracy is a virtue for reporters, and the exercise helps make the point that accuracy requires practice. You have to work at being observant. When the students compare notes, they often find their stories vary so much they have to wonder if they were all in the same room.

I've found it takes practice to notice what God is doing in my life. I have to work at it. I have to take time for reflection, to ponder things that happen and ask, "How is God in this? What am I supposed to learn here?"

When Clint was eleven years old, Mary went away overnight to visit a friend, so it fell to my lot to get him up and ready for school. After he left, I sat in the kitchen cuddling a cup of coffee and pondering the process of growing up. Clint, I concluded, would eventually begin to take more responsibility for getting himself up and ready in the morning. I shouldn't be too hard on him.

Just then the phone rang, and a boy who lived several houses up the street asked for Mrs. Wilson. "She's not home," I said. "Can I take a message?"

"I missed the bus," I heard him say, noticing now the worried tone. "And I don't have any way to get to school."

I hesitated for only a second, then told him, "Hold on, Peter! I'll be right there." My duty was clear. I couldn't just let the boy sit there. Besides it was raining. So with surprisingly good grace, I hopped in the truck, picked up Peter, and took him to school.

Later over the last cup in the pot, I thought about the thousands of kids whose parents—or more likely, parent—for one reason or another aren't there for them. If they miss the bus, they call a neighbor. When they skin a knee after school, they wipe their own tears. When some other kid is mean or they miss a place on the team or life just gets too much, they stuff it down and go on. They're forced to fend for themselves. Some grow up with a deep sense of abandonment and an inability to trust anyone except themselves.

Fortunately while Mary was a widow, she was able to stay home and be there for her children, and wisely she chose to do that. On occasion it seems to me she errs on the side of overprotection, but that morning I heard God say to me, "That's okay. Clint will learn. He'll be on his own soon enough. He'll set his alarm clock, make his lunch, get to school or work on time. Lighten up, Ron! Let him be a boy."

I might not have made this observation a year or two ago, but I'm learning. I'm getting a little better at finding God in the middle of phone calls and interruptions and seemingly chance incidents. I'm looking at the details and asking what he's trying to tell me. I'm practicing and developing my powers of observation, and I'm seeing God work.

I wonder, at some other time would I have told Peter, "Sorry! I'm working. I'm writing a book about watching God work and about caring for people."

I remember a similar response I had years ago. I was reading a humorous book called *The Gospel Blimp*, about a group of Christians who rent a blimp to fly over their neighborhood and drop tracts telling their neighbors about Jesus. I had just read the part about a tract falling into a neighbor's glass of beer as he sat in his backyard when the bell rang and my landlord came in to fix a faulty electrical outlet. This man was a nonstop talker if you gave him a chance, so I disengaged. I kept my nose in the book hoping he wouldn't begin a conversation. Only later, amazed and in disbelief that I could have so blatantly missed the point of the book, did I ask God to forgive me. God had given me an opportunity to get to know my neighbor, and I blew it. He was working around me, and I didn't notice. My powers of observation of God were not too highly developed.

I've had a little practice since then. Today I trust I'd get the point of the book. As I try to see God and hear him in the commonplace, it's amazing what sights I see.

To see God in the ordinary requires not just practice but determination. It means focusing, asking yourself God questions, pondering the events around you in the light of what else you know about God.

Author Frederick Buechner often urges people to "pay attention to life." Buechner tells about driving regularly from his home in the country to Rutland, Vermont, about forty miles away. He had to pass through the small town of Wallingford, and often as he drove he would ask himself, "Have I passed Wallingford yet?" Apparently he drove much of the trip in that mechanical, mind-wandering way that we all know. He was bent on reaching a goal, oblivious to the moment—which is how many of us pass our days.

"Listen to your life," Buechner writes in his autobiographical work *Now and Then*. "See it for the fathomless mystery that it is. In the boredom and pain of it no less than the excitement and gladness: touch, taste, smell your way to the holy and hidden heart of it. . . ." And I would add, "See God at work."

Several centuries ago when Jean-Pierre de Caussade wrote about "the sacrament of the present moment," he explained to a group of nuns in his charge, "You are searching for God, the idea of God in his essential being. You seek perfection and it lies in everything that happens to you—your suffering, your actions, your impulses are the mysteries under which God reveals himself to you" *(Sacrament)*. Each moment is a moment God has given us, and it is there, in that place, and no place else, that we will at that moment find him.

While digging through some old notes, I discovered I had experienced and written something in a similar vein many years ago. I had volunteered to photograph a piece of woodland that was being set aside as a nature preserve. On an early November morning after a light snow, I stalked the fields and hills and streams, aiming, focusing, shooting, jockeying for better composition, varying the depth of field. And all the time I was seeing the world through a viewfinder.

As I stopped to rest for a moment, I caught sight of a juniper tree with hundreds of soft blue, berrylike cones. It was an astonishing sight, lit as it was by the sun reflecting off the snow, and I immediately put my camera to my eye to capture it for the world to see. Just as I did, however, the wonder of the moment disappeared. And try as I might, I could not regain that first inspiration and sense of awe. A sadder and wiser man, I put my camera down and vowed I would never take another picture until I heard God speak to me through that part of his creation.

Will I ever learn? Do I pay any more attention to each moment today? Do I recognize them as God-given? Does the innocence of a child's smile deepen my joy? Do I see God at work in the tangle of downtown traffic? Do I smell the grass and the dogwood and the rain? Have I passed Wallingford—and did I see God there?

I have found it instructive and rewarding to try and step aside, so to speak, and watch God work around me and in me. And seeing what I believe is the evidence of his hand, especially as it shapes, molds, and polishes me, I am humbled and lifted up, and I am encouraged to give him more room to work.

It's true that we have only a very limited view of God working. Our vision is limited to one infinitesimal part of the whole. A reviewer of Elisabeth Elliot's novel *No Graven Image* carped that the author showed a limited knowledge of what God was doing. "Can you imagine," Mrs. Elliot responded in amazement, "thinking you can find out what God is doing in any place?" We have but a brief and clouded glimpse of God at work, but it's enough.

I once had a file folder in my drawer marked "God Works in a Chinese Restaurant." It was the whimsical working title I had given to an experience I wanted to write about. Mary and Clint and I had lunch after church one Sunday at a place called "The Ming Dynasty," and something happened there in which I recognized God's hand. But months later when I picked up the folder, my sheet of notes was gone, and I never found them. Nor, in spite of hard trying, could I recall the incident. So I was left with a sadness that I had lost one of those moments of my life in which I clearly saw God at work. It isn't easy to pay attention to what God is doing and as a routine affair see him working. I have to work at it. So I prize those moments as Clint prizes his baseball cards. He collects and sorts them, lays them out and looks at them, then puts them away carefully in a shoe box. I begrudge losing one of my memories of God working in my life and knowing I'll never be able to pull it out of the box again and enjoy it.

A friend told me a wonderful story about a bus driver who spent most of his summer driving kids back and forth from a camp in Colorado to their homes in the East. He'd deliver one group to camp, then take another home, let's say, to North Carolina. Next he'd pick up a group in Richmond, and by the time they arrived at camp, it was time for the last group to leave. Back and forth he went, day and night, throughout the summer.

Late one night while most of his passengers slept, he pulled into a roadside cafe for a cup of coffee. When he got back on the bus, however, he had a problem. Embarrassed, he had to wake someone up and ask, "Which way are we going? East or west?"

I am making progress, slowly. God is there in every moment; I'm confident of that. And I believe I'll enjoy the journey more and have more to tell when I get home if I pay more attention, asking God to reveal himself as I pass through the Wallingfords of my life.

Annie Dillard, one of my favorite authors, has unusual powers of observation. Her descriptions of surroundings, especially of nature, raise unforgettable images in my mind. In her book *Pilgrim at Tinker Creek*, she tells about a childhood game in which she "hid" a penny on the sidewalk for someone to find. Then she went away thinking about the "lucky passer-by who would receive in this way, regardless of merit, a free gift from the universe."

"There are lots of things to see," she writes, "unwrapped gifts and free surprises. The world is fairly studded and strewn with pennies cast broadside from a generous hand. But—and this is the point—who gets excited by a mere penny? If you follow one arrow, if you crouch motionless on a bank to watch a tremulous ripple thrill on the water and are rewarded by the sight of a muskrat kit paddling from its den, will you count that a chip of copper only, and go your rueful way? It is dire poverty indeed when a man is so malnourished and fatigued that he won't stoop to pick up a penny. But if you cultivate a healthy poverty and simplicity, so that finding a penny will literally make your day, then, since the world is in fact planted in pennies, you have with your poverty bought a lifetime of days." And then she adds, "What you see is what you get."

As for me, I can find all the evidence I'll ever need of God's love, mercy, power, goodness, and grace, if I keep my eyes open. If I cultivate the habit of watching for these "pennies cast broadside," they make my day. Of course there are exceptions, places where the spiritual pollution is so thick, you need special goggles to see God.

God Works on Bourbon St.

Finding God in the Dark

The first time I walked down Bourbon St. in New Orleans, I went away disappointed and sad. I had heard it was the heart of the French Quarter, which is the heart of old New Orleans. But whatever it once was, the narrow old street is now ruled by the merchants of sleaze. T-shirt shops and strip shows compete for business with bars and cotton candy stands. Tipsy conventioneers in party dress slurp beer from plastic cups and jostle each other as they make their way from one tawdry establishment to the next. Occasionally, as though to recall the past, the sweet sound of a saxophone or a muted trumpet floats from a cafe, and small boys with taps tied to their tennis shoes beat a rhythm on the pavement and beg spare coins from passersby.

There are other sides of New Orleans, however, that I've grown to love. While the Quarter has a certain grace and charm, I've found the city is much more than this old rectangle of narrow streets and tourist traps. Some of God's most gifted sons and daughters have created their works in the Crescent City, so named because it sits in a bend of the Mississippi River. The architecture, the food, the music, the history, the drama, and the literature spawned there make it, for me, a stimulating place to visit. A creative spirit rises in me as I walk by the Greek Revival mansions in the Garden District, or sit by the park in Jackson Square and listen to the best or the worst of the local musicians, or consume the traditional Monday plate of red beans and rice with spicy andouille sausage. This intriguing city piqued the interest of William Faulkner, Tennessee Williams, and Walker Percy. It bred jazz in its back alleys and saloons and developed a well-deserved reputation as a culinary capital.

Mary and I spent a weekend in New Orleans one year shortly before Mardi Gras, which means Fat Tuesday. The city was preparing for the parades, feasts, and balls that precede Ash Wednesday, the first day of Lent, and the carnival—literally, farewell to the flesh—atmosphere was building. After all, the city's unofficial motto is "Let the good times roll."

I wondered in those few days as I sat in the Cafe du Monde munching beignets if it was harder to find God in the midst of decadence than it was, say, in the mountains of Colorado or in a wheat field in Kansas or even in the splendor of the Notre Dame cathedral. I sensed it would be easier to lose sight of God in New Orleans than in many places. The city presses on the visitor a spirit of "let it all out," release inhibitions, give way to whatever impulse moves you. But what about seeing God work in New Orleans? Could I sense his presence on Bourbon St. or in the voodoo souvenir shops or while stuffing down the last, rich bite of rum-laced bread pudding on top of shrimp etouffee?

As the city prepared for the final week of partying and for thousands of visitors, many of the motels and shops had slapped on a fresh coat of paint. Streamers of purple, green, and yellow, the official Mardi Gras colors, hung from the balconies in the French Quarter. Costume shops were pregnant with the rush of business to come. We felt the stirring of the festival atmosphere that would soon grip even the most sober visitors and residents.

From one of the city's tourist brochures I was reminded that Lent represents the forty days in which the Lord fasted in the wilderness. The idea is that before that prolonged period of delayed gratification, you feast and celebrate and give way to the urges of the flesh. Then early on Ash Wednesday morning, you join the crowds of penitents who form lines outside the churches to receive the sign of the cross with a black smudge on your forehead. In that atmosphere, I wondered, is it harder to hear the Spirit who restrains us, warns us when we're at the edge, whispers when we pass from license to licentiousness?

Our home in Virginia sits in sight of the Blue Ridge Mountains. A stand of woods, a pond, and a hay field isolate it from nearby homes and traffic, and grant protection to an occasional deer or wild turkey that wanders indifferently in sight of our windows. It summons images of Eden, and I've often thought that if I can't hear God there, I can't hear him anyplace.

In recent years I've visited a number of missionaries in the difficult, sometimes even sinister, settings to which God called them. Martin and Angela in Tai Chung, Taiwan, for example, lived a half block from a storefront Buddhist temple that opened up onto their narrow street. When the breeze was right, the sweet odor of incense burned to idols floated through the open grates into their apartment.

Smokey Mountain, the infamous garbage dump in Manila where some 18,000 squatters lived and earned a living from rotting refuse, was the most unlikely place in the world, as I saw it, to find God. Lorrie and Joke, who lived just blocks from this stinking, mushy mound, rescued the malnourished and diseased children they found there and nursed them back to health. At times the two women waded through knee-deep sewerage to get to the dump, and when I visited them, Lorrie had already had two bouts with typhoid.

Is it possible to walk in perfect peace and with a full sense of the presence of God in such surroundings? The answer is obviously yes! Lorrie and Joke referred to the fetid heap as "the Promised Land," and their home, in which they housed a dozen or more children and ministered to their mothers, radiated the kind of love and peace that comes only from God. Martin and Angela carried on their work with students with a kind of godly confidence. These Christian workers provided an ample answer to the question I pondered that day in New Orleans. In spite of, or perhaps because of, their seemingly godless surroundings, they sought and found fellowship with God. As the worst of the fallen world pressed in on their eyes, ears, and nostrils, they communed with the Almighty. They aptly illustrate the truth that de Caussade writes about in *The Sacrament of the Present Moment:* "We love God partly for his gifts," and "if they are no longer visible we come to love him for himself alone. . . . Wonderful mystery of love! To deprive a heart of God that longs only for him." What a test of our love—to find God in those places where his image is marred in the lives of strangers, where his creation has been blemished, and where his name is spoken mostly in vain.

The truth is the kingdom of God is in me, not in my environment. I don't need the isolation and quietude of my study or the company of saints or the stillness of a house of God to hear God speak, although such surroundings can aid the process. "My kingdom is not of this world," Jesus told Pontius Pilate (John 18:36). This hurt-filled and calamity-ridden world is fallen. We once knew a pleasing peace and order—in the Garden. Then, like a child banging his fist on the keys of a piano, Eden's perfect harmony became a shrill, discordant noise. Now we, pounding the keys to get our own way, continue the cacophony of sin which blocks out the voice of God.

This process of watching God work in my life and in others' lives is also the process of finding the kingdom of God. The kingdom is not reserved for mountain tops or Sunday mornings. It is not an otherworldliness, an escape from the ugly, unpleasant, hurtful realities of this world. It is here and now in my life and in the lives of those who love him. It is on Bourbon St. and in Manila's garbage dump and in millions of seemingly degenerate corners of the earth.

New Orleans, one guidebook suggests, has more churches (and barrooms, I add) per capita than any other American city. I'm glad. That means more places for God's people to gather and worship together. But don't be fooled. God doesn't live in those wood and stone buildings. He doesn't live on Bourbon St. or in the Blue Ridge Mountains or in the midst of the most awesome splendor that he himself created. He lives in the hearts of those who love him. But I still had a lot to learn about that.

The View from the Piano Bench

Seeing God in Others' Lives

I arrived at the Jones' house a few minutes before the appointed time for the meeting and claimed the piano bench as my roost for the evening. Having to sit up straight on a hard surface might keep me awake, I thought. The small living room was half filled, and I looked around, nodding and mumbling greetings to each person. Three women had settled on the sofa to my right, and as I turned to say hello, my mind went blank. I reached for their names but couldn't pull out even one, so I smiled and chirped, "Hi!" to cover my embarrassment.

The incident nagged me throughout the evening. Why couldn't I recall their names? Had I ever spoken to them? Had I ever addressed them as Shirley or Sandy or Dorothy? I had been in meetings with all three a half dozen times before and had no excuse.

Slowly the unpleasant truth bared itself. Not only could I not remember their names, but I knew almost nothing about them. I didn't know their children's names or whether they even had children. I didn't know their past, their problems, their interests, where they lived, or why they were on this committee. And the ugliest truth of all was that I didn't know because I hadn't cared enough to learn.

Watching God work in this world means seeing him in the lives of others, not just my own. It means seeing others as more than members of a committee or clerks or employees or employers or in any other role. It means being aware that casual acquaintances as well as close friends and family and colleagues bear the image of God. It means caring enough to know about their lives, jobs, joys, pains, problems, and much, much more. And finally it means the intersection of our lives is more than an odd accident. God is in it. And his perfect will for me at that moment means finding Jesus in the face and form of each soul he brings into my life.

Mother Teresa mastered this art among the outcasts and untouchables of Calcutta. Daily she came across them in the streets, dying and diseased, an overpowering stench coming from their festering sores. She picked them up, carried them to her Home for Dying Destitutes, washed them, cared for them, and loved them. And her ability to care for them as though they were Jesus himself often infected those who spent time around her. Malcolm Muggeridge, in *Something Beautiful for God,* writes that as he first saw these offensive creatures, he experienced horror mixed with pity, then compassion. But next he experienced "an awareness that these dying and derelict men and women, these lepers with stumps instead of hands, these unwanted children, were not pitiable, repulsive or forlorn, but rather, dear and delightful; as it might be, friends of longstanding, brothers and sisters." And then the key to it, "the very heart and mystery of the Christian faith," as he puts it: "To soothe those battered old heads, to grasp those poor stumps, to take in one's arms those children consigned to dustbins, because it is his head, and they are his stumps and his children, of whom he said that whosoever received one such child in his name received him."

Occasionally on the streets of a Third World city I have seen such as those he writes about. But most of those who come into my life are, by comparison, the beautiful people. So I figure if Mother Teresa can see Jesus in the most repulsive of these derelicts, it shouldn't be so difficult for me to find him in those who inhabit my life.

Shortly before the piano bench incident a friend asked me if I would accept the nomination to the office of church elder, so I read the description for the job in *The Book of Church Order*. "The elder is informed and aware of the needs of God's people and responds to those needs in the same caring fashion as a shepherd would for his own sheep." That evening sitting on the piano bench I knew that whether or not God wanted me to bear the title, he still wanted me to practice the calling. I had not always done that very well, but it wasn't too late to start.

Finding God in each life that touches ours means first of all being aware. It means breaking out of our own bubble and being sensitive to the fact that the warm human bodies in our proximity, close friends or strangers, are God's creatures with beating, loving, caring, hurting hearts.

For a short time during the later years of my marriage to Carole, we visited a counselor to help improve our communication. Kindly but firmly the counselor said to me, "Ron, listen! When Carole says something, ask yourself what she's saying. Where is she? What's going on underneath?" What the counselor was really telling me was that I was often so preoccupied with my own world I was not aware of the one closest to me. And on reflection I realize if that were true, I was probably even less aware of the casual acquaintance or stranger who entered my life. When we are aware that those around us are deeply feeling, complex, loving, hurting, needy creatures made in the image of God, and they are there by more than chance, it changes the filter through which we see the entire human landscape.

I've often envied those who always seem to have the right question to draw others out. They easily engage a waiter or waitress in conversation or walk up to a total stranger at a party and shine a soft, comfortable spotlight on that person. They seem to be drawn to other people and find their fulfillment in relationships. Personality tests, however, have clearly labeled me an introvert. Gregarious I'm not. Give me a cabin in the woods for a week and I'm close to heaven. At a party I choose one person at a time to talk to—preferably someone I know and in a quiet corner. I don't easily entertain a group or engage strangers in conversation. But this doesn't excuse me from seeking the reflection of the Almighty in the face of each one he puts in my path.

For a number of years I wrote copy for fund appeal letters for various organizations. The organization or its agency sent me a packet of material—background on the organization, examples of their work, a good, gut-wrenching story or two—and I fashioned this material into a letter designed to extract the greatest gift from the giver that good copywriting could wrest. Whether or not this is an honorable profession is another matter, but I soon learned that certain techniques and phrases, words or emphases, could make a 2 or 3 percent difference in the response and this could translate into thousands of dollars. Touch this hot button and bingo. Use this device or that method and 158 more people will put a check in the return envelope.

Knowing how easy it was to manipulate words and phrases to get the desired response, it was difficult not to depersonalize the process, even though the successful fund appeal letter is one that appears to be a personal letter, written directly to each of the thousands of names on the mailing list. It was at this point I wrote my last letter, vowed I'd never write another, and turned my skills toward some other form of writing. If I had to blot from my mind the spark of the divine that I believed was native to my readers and practice a kind of literary trickery to earn a living, I'd sooner go on welfare.

This recognition of God in the lives of others, as well as in our own, will determine to a great extent *how* we respond to them. I've traveled to Latin America a number of times in recent years, and each time I promise myself I won't go again until I've improved my Spanish. My lack of the language leads to some comic but frustrating situations. At the restaurant in a hotel in Guatemala City where I stayed for a week, I ordered cafe au lait each morning. I've grown to enjoy the strong black coffee mixed with hot milk, which is a staple of breakfast in many countries. The coffee and the milk are often served in separate, small metal pots, and you can mix it to your taste.

On the first morning, the waitress brought the black coffee, then went away. Ten minutes later when the coffee had cooled, she brought the milk. The next morning she brought the milk first, and when that was lukewarm, she brought the coffee. The third morning I tried in my halting Spanish to suggest it would be nice if she brought both at the same time, but to no avail. By the fourth day I knew I was getting nowhere.

Not being able to say what you want in a language, however, also curbs a sharp tongue. I confess that a few pointed comments crossed my mind, but fortunately I couldn't express those in Spanish. And that's when it occurred to me that it was more important that I reflect the love of Christ in my response to this woman than it was that I have a cup of hot coffee. It's more important for me to treat each person in my life as someone special in God's sight than it is for me to get what I want from that person at the moment. No matter the other's conduct, my call is to see the likeness of Christ someplace underneath.

Let's face it, though; some people are harder to like than others. The likeness of Christ is well-hidden under less than Christ-like behavior, and we do no good to deny it. If we are to find God in the lives of others, we have to see them realistically, not as plaster saints when they're real sinners. Instead we have to forgive their sins—and that puts our Christianity to the test. I have often glibly quoted the biblical admonition "Bear ye one another's burdens, and so fulfill the law of Christ" (Gal. 6:2 KJV), without realizing that, as Dietrich Bonhoeffer writes in *A Testament to Freedom*, "my brother's burden which I must bear is not only his outward lot, his natural characteristics and gifts, but quite literally his sin. And the only way to bear that sin is by forgiving it in the power of the cross of Christ in which I now share." "Forgiveness," Bonhoeffer added, "is the Christ-like suffering which it is the Christian's duty to bear."

Pity the disciples who failed to see the image of God in the children brought to Jesus for his blessing. In the face of a child, perhaps, it is easiest, although I confess others are quicker to do this than I am. Mary, for example, instinctively brightens up and turns on when a child appears. Put a three-year-old or a nine-year-old in her path, and the light literally shines in her eyes. And it appears as though she has passed on this grace to Amy, Mike, and Clint.

One summer evening at dusk Mary and I sat on the front porch with our friends the Howards. Their children, three lively girls ages four, seven, and nine at the time, were cavorting on the front lawn, aided and abetted by Amy and Mike, both college students, and Clint, then twelve. Actually it was just as much fun to watch the older ones playing with the children. They were leading the girls on a frog hunt, promising to make green Kool-Aid if they could find one.

"It's unusual," a friend had said on a similar occasion, "to see young people that age so interested in small children." But I had seen it often. Mike, six-foot-two, broad shouldered and generally reserved, melts when the Howard girls come to visit. Amy has a countywide reputation as a baby-sitter and a client list that keeps her constantly booked. Clint, who often volunteers to work in the nursery, has a natural, easy manner that draws small children to him and he to them.

From my perch on the piano bench that night I saw something in the faces of my friends and in my own heart that I had never seen before. And it reminded me of the view that Tolstoy's Martuin Avdyeitch had from the cobbler's bench in his basement shop. Martuin could see only feet and lower legs passing by, but he often recognized the passerby by the boots that he, Martuin, had made or repaired.

Martuin had a dream one night in which he heard the Lord say to him, "Be on the watch. I am coming to visit you tomorrow." So the next day he put on the tea kettle and the cabbage soup and settled at his work bench with one eye on his work and another on those passing by.

Three times that day his work was interrupted by people passing by who had some problem or other. An old man shoveling snow, a young woman in flimsy summer clothes with a small child, an old apple woman chasing a boy who had stolen an apple. Martuin invited the first two in for tea, gave the young woman a coat and twenty kopeks, and made peace between the boy and the apple woman. And so his day went until it began to get dark and Martuin cleaned up his bench, put the tea kettle on again, and took down his New Testament to read. It was then he heard the voices in the corner—the old man, the young woman and the child, and the old lady. "Did you not recognize me, Martuin?" the voice said. "It was I." And at the same time Martuin's eye fell on the page in the Bible where he read, "For I was an hungred, and ye gave me meat: I was thirsty, and ye gave me drink: I was a stranger, and ye took me in. . . . Inasmuch as ye have done it unto one of the least of these my brethren, ye have done it unto me" (Matt. 25:35, 40 KJV). And Martuin's soul rejoiced.

'Tis a Gift to Be Simple

The Undivided Heart

If I listen, I can hear Sheila's flute, the strains of the old Shaker tune "Simple Gifts" floating in the humid air under the canopy. And I can hear Ann's bell-clear tones as she sings, "'Tis a gift to be simple; 'tis a gift to be free." Mary and I asked them to play and sing this piece during our wedding ceremony, and even as the morning edged toward a sticky ninety-four degrees, I shivered slightly, and I do again as I recall it.

We chose this piece because we both had expressed a desire to understand true simplicity and make it not just a part of our lives but a theme of our relationship. We were quick, and still are, to confess we didn't know what that meant or would mean. In fact we were sure, and still are, that we don't fully understand what simplicity really is. We suspected then, and now we are sure, that it wouldn't be easy to discover the meaning of it nor would it be easy to practice what little we might discover.

I would love to have an electric motor operated by a foot pedal to run my twelve-foot fishing boat. I find great enjoyment, therapy even, in sitting in the boat casting around the water and occasionally catching a one- or two-pound bass. Often on a sunny day I have sat in the boat on a pond or river without a single nibble. Yet I didn't care. The tranquility and the escape from the tyranny of the immediate made it worthwhile.

Over the years I've acquired two comfortable seats for the boat, a gaggle of rods and tackle, and an electric trolling motor that I operate with one hand while I fish with the other. It's a modest outfit as fishing outfits go, and a motor operated by pedals would be a small improvement, the next logical step to upgrading the outfit. But I don't *need* it. I would simply enjoy it if I had it.

About a year ago I persuaded myself that it would make a fine birthday gift and I deserved it. It would be good for me, and it would maximize the therapy. So I'd make myself a present. But when the time came, I realized the rationalization for what it was, and I passed. I also realized the motor represented more clutter that could obscure my vision of God. If I could persuade myself to buy the motor, I could easily persuade myself to buy a slightly larger boat, new seats, better rods, and on and on. If my boat was stolen or sunk, I'd be disappointed, but I believe I could praise God and allow the loss to draw me closer to him. If I had bought the electric motor and something happened to it, I suspect I would have a much more difficult time seeing God in the middle of it.

Possessions can quickly complicate life. It is not just a truism to say that the less we have, the less we have to worry about. It is the essence of simplicity. Buy an electric motor and you need a battery. Buy a battery and you need a battery charger. Pretty soon you'll want a trailer to carry it, and you'll need insurance and registration for the trailer. Life was much simpler when I paddled the boat. In fact, when I took up fishing ten years ago, I fished from the bank of the river, and I had a good time. Then I bought a one-person canoe and paddled up and down the river. Next I traded the canoe plus 100 dollars for the jon boat. So what's next after a foot-pedal motor? Perhaps one of these slick jobs with raised seats and a well in which to put the fish I catch and a 200 horsepower outboard motor to help me fly across the lake at fifty mph? If we don't have possessions, we can't worship them. If I don't have a boat, I can't make it into an idol that I put before God. It's no sin to have a boat—but it is dangerous.

This relationship between the comfort of material goods and spiritual growth is clear in Scripture. It's easier to trust in what is seen than in the unseen. So the more we have, the easier it is to trust in it and not in God. (Wealth is relative, I know, but if you can afford to buy this book and have the leisure time to read it, chances are you're rich like me.) Unless we sell all we have, we have to deal with this question of continuing to trust God in the midst of our comfort.

Several years ago I visited a poor, coal-mining town in Kentucky to do a story on a group of Mother Teresa's Sisters of Charity who were working there. They had bought a modest house on a side street, and neighbors told me that before they moved in, they pulled out the wall-to-wall carpeting and gave away the washer and dryer. Each nun had only one change of clothes and slept on a mat. Not only did these Christian workers identify with the poor that way, but by stripping down to the bare necessities they had less to distract them from God.

If it's true, then, that the assorted extras we've collected along the way complicate the Christian life, why don't we sell everything we have and give the money to the poor? God has obviously called some to do this. It appears that the rich ruler whom Jesus told to sell all he had was too attached to his wealth. Jesus knew it and put to him the test of obedience. I pray if God asks the same of me I'll hear the message. And while he may not require me to sell my boat, he does demand that I don't get too attached to it.

Voluntary poverty, of course, is not an end in itself. It earns nothing. Downward mobility may clear the channel so we can see the image of God and hear the sound of his voice a little better. But it doesn't impress God. Simplicity consists neither in the quantity of goods we do or don't possess nor in the amount of attention, or lack thereof, that we give to them.

Simplicity is, first of all, an attitude of the heart that says nothing I possess really belongs to me, nor will it last forever. It is the opposite of duplicity, which, it seems to me, is more the human condition. Duplicity is thinking one thing and saying another. It's covering your intentions with false moves or words. It's dividing your allegiance, wanting to put God before everything else but being unwilling to let go of some things. It was described well by the psalmist who prayed, "Give me an undivided heart, that I may fear your name" (Ps. 86:11). An undivided heart has one goal, one love. With an undivided heart I'm not split between what I want and what God wants for me. I want what God wants. Reduced to a simple description, then, simplicity is this: Seek first the kingdom of God and all these things will be given to you. We hadn't made this analysis at the time, but Mary and I had the reference for this Scripture, Matthew 6:33, inscribed inside our wedding bands.

I wouldn't want you to think we have even begun to understand or achieve a state of simplicity. I write now in a confessional mode. Neither in attitude nor in practice have I come close to the goal God has for me. Mary and I still struggle with the details of what we buy, what we sell, what we need, what we don't need. We'll always do that, I'm sure. But we both believe simplicity is a gift from God as well as a discipline. So we'll ask God to help us recognize it when we see it and—what is even more difficult at times—obey him when we do.

A pedal-operated electric motor may symbolize for me a level of luxury, but it's only the tip of the iceberg, the 10 percent that rises above a deep sea of desires. If I could see clearly beneath the surface, it would probably scare the life out of me.

A funny thing happened not long ago. A friend of mine wanted to sell a small fishing boat with a pedal-operated motor, a trailer, a depth finder, and a lot of other gear. I knew I couldn't afford it, but I offered to fix it up and sell it, thinking perhaps I could work some kind of a deal to buy the motor. I hauled the whole rig to my house and found first that the motor needed repair. "And it's not worth the money," they told me at a local repair shop. "You can buy a used one just as cheap."

"Do you have a used one?" The old desire raised its ugly head.

"I'm working on one now," I was told.

"Well, call me when you get it done. I'm really interested," I said, and I left the shop, visions of hands-free fishing floating in my head.

That was a long time ago. The repair man never called, and I still don't have a pedal-operated motor. Which is okay. In fact it would be okay if I had to go back to fishing from the bank of the river. Life was a lot simpler then.

Finding God at the Bijou

"Whatever is pure . . .
think about such things"

The critics gushed over the film: "Uproariously funny . . . great entertainment . . . you'll laugh your sides off." Well, that's what I needed. Something light. I usually go more for drama and suspense at the movies, but I thought this would give me a break from mourning. There was just one problem—it was rated R. I had learned years ago that I was very uncomfortable with the level of violence or sex in most R-rated films, and as a rule I avoided them. But this was a comedy. How much sex and violence could they inject into a funny film?

A lot, I soon found out. It was mostly the language. As the film went on, the profanity and vulgarity rose to the point that I physically cringed. Rarely had I heard the level of obscenity that fouled the air of that theater, and I had spent two years in the army. I lasted less than an hour, and I should have left sooner. But finally I picked up my popcorn, hauled myself from the chair, and almost ran for the refuge of the lobby.

The incident raised many questions for which I've found no easy answers. I love the vicarious experience of a well-written and acted film. With the lights out and the figures larger than life on a big screen, I can lose myself for two hours in a world other than my own. A good piece of fiction can have the same result. Or a well-staged musical or a play. Even a TV sitcom, for that matter, can bring a healthy relief from the real stresses of the moment by evoking a range of emotions, from amusement to fear, through imaginary situations.

Fantasy has value. Escape is legitimate. Entertainment can enhance the quality of life. The unlimited combinations of imagination and emotion, words and images, in film, stage performance, and writing can lift our spirits, lead us to praise and thankfulness, and rouse reflections on truth. Unfortunately, much of the entertainment that initially attracts me turns out to be marred by images and ideas that repulse me and leave me feeling dirty. The constant drumming of scatological words and phrases in that so-called comedy left me disgusted. They debased human sexual relations and left a stench in my mind. And there is nothing comical about that.

Entertainment can take us up or take us down. And it's not just commercially motivated schlock that is saturated with intimate bedroom antics or shocking brutality. So many well-crafted novels, brilliantly acted plays and films, cleverly written, even artfully performed musicals are spoiled for me by an excess of obscene dialogue or deviant sexual themes or a parade of mutilated corpses or altogether too-realistic enactments of torture, beatings, and stabbings. How many people can I see shot or dismembered, or how much careless copulation can I consider without clouding the image of the good and the true and the beautiful? How much can I fill my mind with the vile and the ugly and with themes of despair without crowding out God? It is next to impossible, I believe, to find God working in the ordinary events of life while we are enjoying images and ideas that he would not enjoy. "Whatever is true, whatever is noble, whatever is right, whatever is pure, whatever is lovely, whatever is admirable—if anything is excellent or praiseworthy," Paul writes, "think about such things" (Phil. 4:8).

It's worth noting that many who make no particular claims to speak as Christians nor cite Scripture as their authority have some of the same, uneasy feelings. Newspaper columnist Ellen Goodman wrote about the lack of censorship on the part of the TV networks of vulgar expressions and words that male television anchors had to practice saying before a mirror before they could bring themselves to say on camera. "We seem to be in this fluid error," she writes, "where any number of formerly dirty words are being washed clean. At the same time, formerly acceptable terms have become fighting words."

All this has led me to several conclusions.

First, I live in the world. I don't want to escape it at the moment, nor should I. Some have chosen that route. A friend of mine told me that as a small boy he told his mother he wanted to go to church that night because the missionary was showing slides. "Okay," his mother allowed reluctantly, but as he left she admonished him, "If those pictures start to move, you come right on home."

Secondly, my thought life shapes what I am, and I am responsible for it. As difficult as it is to break away from the verbal and visual squalor around me, I must. It takes great effort to escape the orgy of sexual excess or sort out the uplifting from the degrading messages that infringe on our solitude. The lead actor in the film I walked out on had a great ability to make me laugh at something that, upon reflection, I knew I shouldn't laugh at. He was a short, pudgy man with an amazing ability to contort his facial expressions. And he was naturally funny, with a quick wit and a precise sense of timing. Unfortunately he used these gifts to humiliate others or demean them with lewd remarks.

As happened here, I occasionally find myself laughing at something that I know I shouldn't. But I laugh spontaneously before something can be screened by my mind and be rejected as vulgar, obscene, or profane. In such cases we don't have a chance to say, "No! This doesn't please God. I won't laugh." (How can you ask before laughing, "Would Jesus laugh at this?")

If I spend too much time in the barn, I can expect to get manure on me. It's my own fault. From experience I know that certain writers, film directors, or comedians have a reputation for vulgarity, obscenity, or violence. So wisdom dictates that I avoid them.

Does this mean I have to unplug the television, read only the books sold in religious bookstores, and watch only G-rated films? I don't think so. But it does mean I have to use the on-off button on the TV, close the sullied book, and head for the theater exit when what I'm watching or reading begins to push God out of my mind.

I had no need to leave early when I went to see the stage musical *Blood Brothers*. This is a sad story of twins separated at birth. The mother, destitute and despairing, gives one of the brothers to an upper-class woman who raises him without telling him about his natural mother.

I saw the show while in London, and as I pushed my way through the theater crowds on Charing Cross Road after the performance, my mind ran back over the scenes. How clearly the story had illustrated the privileges of class and the lack of choices of the poor.

And it also carried the message that we are responsible for our actions. They have consequences. The dialogue occasionally lapsed into four-letter words, but I didn't feel dirty or manipulated. The show was well written, well acted, and well staged, and it carried messages consistent with biblical truth. I enjoyed the evening, and I could thank God for it.

Some observers of our culture say the creators of modern entertainment are infatuated with foul language and violence, and these critics bemoan the depths to which our society has fallen. They grumble that it can't get much worse. I think it can, as it has at other times and in other places in history. But I see little value in standing around mourning the demise of a Christian culture or trying to legislate the present one out of existence—if I am personally wallowing in it. If each of us—beginning with me—would clean up our own act, we would have more of an impact on our culture than we can imagine.

Meanwhile this world, as Eugene Peterson writes, "is no friend to grace." There is a war going on out there for my soul. Martin Luther wrote about the Christian's battle with the world, the flesh, and the Devil. If I forget this for a moment—and I often do—I stand in danger of being seduced. Mary and I had a lot to learn about this as we began life together.

No Man Is an Island

Learning about the Body of Christ

Skip Ryan had a "worry" chair, as he called it, in his office. It was a comfortable wing-back with blue brocade upholstery and tattered arm rests that overwrought visitors had rubbed until the padding showed through. Often during long months of lip-biting grief, I had slumped in that chair and worn a few more threads bare.

Usually Skip had a timely insight from years of pastoring or from the Scriptures. At other times—he seemed to know just when to do it—he simply sat and listened while I poured out my woes. This time, however, I had happier thoughts to convey. Mary and I had begun to talk seriously about a long-term relationship, and while I couldn't conceive of the possibility that I was making a mistake, Skip was my friend as well as my pastor. I valued his advice, and I suspected he'd have more than just congratulations to offer.

"You know," he said after I had blurted out my news and we had talked awhile, "your relationship with Mary affects more than just the two of you."

"Oh, yes! Of course!" I said. That made sense. My mind reached for the implications, but they eluded me for the moment. I was sure he was right, but as I left his office that day, I had little idea of the extent to which his observation would prove true.

A few weeks later Mary and I had a hint of what Skip meant as we told Mary's children—Amy, Mike, and Clint—and my children—Ken, Heather, and Todd—about our plans. Yes, this would definitely affect them even though three of them were already out of the nest. But it wasn't until months after we were married that we began to grasp the extent to which our decision would modify the lives of many people.

A counselor told us how to draw a geneogram, which is a tool to facilitate marital understanding but could pass for an amusing parlor game. We covered the kitchen table with a large piece of paper and began to draw our family trees, going back several generations and including former spouses. Then we drew lines from one member to another and talked about those relationships. My father's mother, Annette, for example, was a true Victorian who ruled her husband, Herbert, as well as those around her, and in the process earned my mother's undying resentment. Mary's great-grandmother, Nana, abused her granddaughter (Mary's mother), believing she looked like her "no good father, Carl." I was the third of four children, and my older brother Norman was the favored child of my dominating paternal grandmother.

And on it went. Slowly we began to see how these relationships helped to shape who we are, how we brought this history into our marriage, and how they influence us even to this day. We had just hung another branch on those trees and were in the process of profoundly altering the lives of those close to us.

Perhaps our culture's emphasis on individual rights and privacy leads us illogically to believe we can live in a vacuum. Christian isolation is a contradiction of terms. Even my thought life, while thankfully beyond the purview of my friends and family, is not just my business. I'm just a corpuscle—or some other component—in the corpus of Christ. There are no strangers in the kingdom.

When we got married, we decided to live in the house Mary had been living in for ten years. One afternoon we pulled out boxes of family photos, sorted, matted, and framed them, and integrated them on the walls of the play room. We mixed the families and the generations. My mother hangs beside Mary's oldest son. Mary's former spouse shares space with my oldest son at age five. People who have passed on but had never met on earth look benignly from the walls with little hint of how their lives have converged.

John Donne, the seventeenth century English poet and pastor, was right: no man is an island. And Skip was right: Mary and I have had an immediate impact on our families and friends, and the repercussions of our union will reach for many generations to come.

The corollary of Skip's statement is that the actions, examples, words and ideas of others touch and often profoundly affect our lives as well. I'm often surprised by whom God uses to speak to me. And I might be surprised to learn whose life, unknown to me, I have influenced. Of course it shouldn't surprise me. I learned long ago in visiting various cultures, especially in developing countries, that I was touched by those who appeared most unlikely to teach me something. That attitude reflected a paternalism that I picked up no doubt from my own culture.

A few years ago I traveled to the Ansokia Valley in Ethiopia to write about conditions five years after one of the great famines. Some 30,000 people had faced starvation at the time, and a relief group had brought in food and medicine. They set up a station at one end of the valley and for months fed and cared for thousands who were weak and desperate. When the rains returned, the relief organization began a development program to help the people get back on their feet and become self-sufficient.

I wandered up and down the valley for a week, talking to many of the people who had lived through those horrifying days. Many were believers, as were most of the relief and development workers. However, because the government at that time arbitrarily, often cruelly, repressed all signs of religion, the small group of believers worshiped underground and were very careful to whom they talked about faith.

I was moved by the devotion of these Christians who had endured so much and still risked so much. I had suffered a few misfortunes in my life but nothing to compare with what they had undergone. Yet I could detect no trace of bitterness in their sweet, refreshing spirit. They could teach me and my friends back home so much about Christian living, I thought. The development workers had given them the means to continue living on earth; but they offered something that was eternal.

On another occasion I remember spending an evening with two close friends. We ate fine food at one of our favorite restaurants and talked among other things about our work, our love life, world peace, college basketball, and God. It was a warm summer evening, and outside in the parking lot we continued our conversation, reluctant to end the fellowship and break the spell. I remarked casually how much of a difference it had made to me many years before when I discovered that I could know God and have a personal, day-by-day relationship with him. I assumed all Christians had made that discovery early in their Christian lives, especially these friends. Months later, however, I was surprised to hear one of them just as casually comment that my remark in the parking lot came as a revelation to him and marked a significant point in his spiritual life.

Skip's comment that day has one other implication that I now see more clearly: It's not just my actions and words that affect others but my very relationship to God affects them too. How I live affects not just what I write, but how God uses that writing. I can't live one kind of life off-line, so to speak, and convey a different message in print. As a part of the body of Christ, I am responsible to keep myself pure and close to God. The parts of a body are mutually dependent, so my holiness, or lack thereof, directly or indirectly affects not just me, but all believers.

Ordinary Sinners

God Works through Our Weakness

I met Russell and Barbara Reid a few months before they left the Philippine island of Mindoro. They had spent forty years there as missionaries to the primitive Tawbuid people. Inspired by stories of pioneer work among unreached people, Russell and Barbara had applied to the China Inland Mission just as that mission's members were being forced off the mainland by the Communists. So when the mission sent them to Mindoro, they were pleased.

Six tribes under the collective name of Mangyan lived in the mountains on the island, and almost no evangelistic work existed among them. Each tribe spoke a different language, and few spoke each other's language or the Philippine language of Tagalog. Little was known about some of the tribes, and it took Russell and Barbara a year and a half before they could even find a village of the Tawbuid, the tribe to which they had been assigned.

For months at a time Russell and Barbara lived in the hills in the same kind of bamboo and palm-leaf huts in which the Tawbuid lived. They hauled water and cooked sweet potatoes over an open fire. They often trekked for days over the mountains, fording rivers, crossing swamps, looking for villages. And later they returned to teach those with whom they had made contact. They raised four children on the island, suffered the heartache of separation when the children left for school, and endured sickness, storms, loneliness, and all the standard difficulties of pioneer mission work. In those forty years they saw a strong church established, Tawbuid young people attend Bible school, and the new believers catch the missionary vision to take the gospel to other villages. The same thing had happened in the other five tribes where other "ordinary" missionaries with extraordinary commitment worked. Once again God chose the weak things of the world to fulfill his purposes.

When I met Russell and Barbara, they were putting the final touches on a Tawbuid translation of the Scriptures, and when that was done, they would return to their native California, and the work of a lifetime would be over.

We talked about their return and how they would share the story of the amazing work God had done on that island. But Barbara had misgivings. "Young people today don't seem to understand that we're not anything special," she protested. "They make us out to be heroes, and they put us on a pedestal. They marvel that anyone would stay in such a place for forty years. They just don't think in such terms. But we're just ordinary people."

She is right. Like most of the missionaries I've met, they had gifts from God, but they weren't outstanding scholars or world-class athletes or award-winning anything. They were average, everyday, bread-and-butter missionaries. What made them extraordinary was their commitment to Christ.

I felt a kinship to Russell and Barbara as I visited them that day. I think of myself as ordinary and have often caught myself looking at the exceptionally talented and gifted people I know with a touch of envy. If only I had his writing skills or imagination or good looks or natural athletic ability or her intellect or education or money, how much I could accomplish! I know, however, that I have exactly the abilities God wants me to have—no more, no less. I don't have to live in the shadow of others. Nor should I envy those who win awards or get their names in lights. What God wants from me is obedience born of love. He requires simply that I use the abilities and resources he has given me—few or many—in the way he directs.

But that isn't easy in a society that values fame and worships celebrities. I am easily seduced by the temptation to be known. I have a small journalism textbook in my study that was written many years ago by a hard-nosed editor turned academic. I took several of his courses in graduate school and asked him to sign the book. To my amazement at the time, he wrote, "You seem like a person who will someday edit, in an important way, a religious publication." I never asked him what he meant by that, but until that time I had never imagined myself as "the editor," and I confess that in considering his prophecy I couldn't help fantasizing about having my name on the top of the masthead of some magazine.

I know God uses the gifts he has given us when we offer them to him, but I also know he delights in working through our weaknesses because that brings glory to him. Throughout history he has chosen those we might vote "most *unlikely* to succeed" for some of the most significant accomplishments in the work of his kingdom. He picked Peter, the fisherman, John Bunyan, the tinker turned preacher, and D. L. Moody, the former shoe salesman, and did great deeds through them. Many other so-called ordinary people through whom God has done extraordinary things never will be known to anyone but God and a handful of others. Chuck Colson tells about going into a prison with a well-known gospel singer and a converted ex-convict. Chuck preached, the singer sang, and the ex-con gave his testimony. But what impressed one inmate the most was a group of women with Colson's party who left the glare of the TV lights and the center of attention and sat down to a meal with a few of the prisoners.

God has obviously given some people exceptional gifts and called many, willingly or unwillingly, to leadership. Many Christians have gained notoriety and public acclaim almost as a by-product of their obedience to God. They sought God, and he used the enormous talents he gave them in a way that put them in the public eye. Theirs is the more difficult path. They have to wrestle with the temptation to believe their own press releases, to conclude they not only achieved fame on their own but somehow deserved it. I have to deal only with the desire for fame and not fame itself.

I have grown more confident in recent years, not in my ability to achieve some kind of socially defined success, but in God's desire to work in and through me and use the gifts he has given me. I have grown to expect more of myself, not because of some sudden determination to show the world or to reach some arbitrary goal, but because I know it is God who works in me. As I have watched God work and discovered with growing amazement his hand in the ordinary events of my life, I have come to understand more of his will and purpose for my life.

Having said this I realize the need to guard against a kind of pride in my humility. It is just one small step from recognizing we are ordinary sinners to being proud of it. A friend once told me about the time he visited a former flower child and prostitute who was in the hospital. John and his wife had taken in this woman's daughter. "I went to the hospital thinking how cool I was to take time out of my day to do this," he told me. Reflecting on the tough life this woman had lived, he asked her, "Barbara, why do you think some people always seem to get the short end of the stick in life?"

She mused for a moment, then replied, "I don't know, John, but I think God won't give us more than we can handle. And I guess some of us can handle more."

"It was like getting hit in the stomach," John told me. "I had galloped in there like the Lone Ranger, and with one innocent remark she ripped off my mask. God had given me a comfortable life with few complications. And I had to ask myself if it was really because I couldn't take the kind of suffering Barbara had had to endure."

Most of us probably think of ourselves as ordinary. Yet none of us have been left with absolutely no abilities God can use.

I heard about one woman who told a prison worker, "You have such a wonderful ministry. All I know how to do is bake chocolate cookies."

The prison worker replied, "Baking chocolate cookies is a ministry. Unless you eat them all yourself, you can give them to people."

ADD *with* H

"Be still and know
that I am God"

You were a squirmer," my mother told me later in life. I was a wiggly kid who couldn't sit still for a minute. More than once she asked me, "Do you have ants in your pants?"

Being my mother, she had more patience with me than my teachers in school, where my restlessness often brought down trouble. Unfortunately, it seems I've never lost the itch. Even today Mary tells me I fidget in church. I shift around and write down extraneous thoughts, and even under the most gripping preaching, I often have to work at paying attention.

I thought about this recently when Mary wrote a paper for a class in learning disabilities. ADD with H, she explained to me, is psychological shorthand for "attention deficit disorder, accompanied by hyperactivity." Some children daydream or talk excessively or interrupt frequently or shift from one activity to another. They don't finish things, or they're impulsive, or they can't seem to play quietly. The experts believe a chemical deficiency in the area of the brain that controls attention, impulsivity, and activity is at the root of the problem for many.

I've found that as people hear about ADD for the first time, the wheels go around and you can almost hear them ask, "Hmmm? I wonder if I had that problem?" I wondered myself! Was this why I struggled with schoolwork, why even today my mind wanders, why I fidget in church, why I have trouble concentrating on a piece of writing for any length of time?

It was interesting speculation, but it struck me that we are all afflicted with a kind of spiritual ADD, often with H. To "discover God in the smallest and most ordinary things," as de Caussade writes, to be aware of the sacrament, that is, the mystery of God's will for us each moment, requires concentration. It's hard work. We are easily distracted. We go for long periods of time—hours, days, even longer for some—without more than perfunctory awareness of God. We are so caught up in our own world we lose sight of the fact that God is working in and around our lives at every moment. If we could only walk through life with this awareness, how much deeper and richer would be our joy and peace.

I've often wondered why I don't think of God more often in my waking hours. What keeps me from praying continually, as Paul instructed the Christians in Thessalonica to do? Why am I not in continual conversation with the Lord, considering that he's always there, ready to listen and answer? Why do I miss the enjoyment and reward that constant fellowship can bring?

The main cause of spiritual Attention Deficit Disorder is, I've concluded, the desire to do what *I* want to do, to manage my own life, to be in control, in short, *to play God.* I call this the "I Did It My Way" syndrome, and it's a universal affliction. The serpent deceived Eve and told her that if she ate from the tree of the knowledge of good and evil, she would be like God. So I spend a good part of my day in self-deception, laboring under the illusion that I have everything in hand. Without any awareness of the leading of the Spirit, I take charge, make decisions, push ahead, run my own life, thinking all the time that I'm doing a half decent job of it.

My propensity to go my own way, thinking I'm in control, is an indication of a lack of trust that God can or will really do it. It's one thing to pray that God will provide a job or care for my children or direct the committee. But I'm still needed, right? Many people grow up in homes where they never feel safe. They don't feel the love and protection of caring parents, so they determine they have to do it themselves. They learned that if they depended on anyone else, they'd get hurt.

If they offered love, they risked rejection. If anyone got to know them well, that person might not like them. So, learning to turn over every care and concern to God in every situation is especially difficult.

My need to feel in control may not be as severe as that of someone who has suffered deep childhood trauma—abandonment or abuse—but I still have trouble completely trusting God, as well as a pesky, underlying urge to do what I want to do, regardless. If I truly trusted God for everything, I'd be seeking the sacrament of each moment, living and breathing an awareness of God, and enjoying the pure pleasure of his presence.

I am very aware that the lack of awareness of the presence of God at all times is at the root of the repetition of my sins. When I come to God with the sorry realization that for the nth time in my Christian life I've committed the same old sin, I know at the time I did the deed I was not in conscious communion with God. When I come with the cry "I've done it again, Lord," I realize that I had pulled down the shade of my mind to keep out the light of God's Word.

I don't like the implications of my spiritual ADD. When I fell in love with Mary, I couldn't think of anything else. While I was trying to read a book, write, shave, do my taxes, or whatever, thoughts of her intruded. I wondered if I'd get anything done. It was terribly distracting—although I enjoyed every minute of it. That love-struck stage eventually passed, but even today she's not far from my mind at any moment. So why don't I think constantly about God, the lover of my soul?

While thoughts of Mary drift in and out of my consciousness without bidding, I have to practice the presence of God. "To be sure," Richard Foster writes in what is probably the best contemporary treatment of the topic, "this life of unbroken fellowship is not automatic or effortless. . . . We do not leap into the dizzy heights of constant communion in a single bound. It comes over a period of time in measured practical steps" *(Prayer)*.

It does, however, please God. And it pleases me. I've experienced great heights of pleasure in many things in life, but none compare with that sense of "all's right with the world" that God has often imparted throughout the day. It is truly, as de Caussade described it, "the sacrament of the present moment."

Again, to be honest, I don't live this way consistently. And even if I did, I certainly don't believe life can be constant bliss. Pain is normal on earth. Disappointment and loss will always be with us. My own inadequacies will get me in trouble. But as far as I'm concerned, what makes it bearable is the foretaste of heaven God allows us in constant communion with him.

A *Declaration of Dependence*

God's Part in Our Growth

I remember when the angel first appeared. It was at Christmastime, several weeks before Carole died. The figure was dressed in a long, flowing blue garment, and it had wings and a trumpet. It was made from papier-mâché and was mounted high on the wall at the front of the church where it commanded the attention of every worshiper. It floated gracefully ahead along the wall toward the window with its trumpet pointing the way, and it brought a lot of comfort to me that season. It was an angel that had shown the apostle John a vision of a place where God will wipe away every tear, where there will be no more death or mourning or crying or pain, and God will be there with his people. So this angel brought just the right message for me at that moment.

The next year a second angel appeared on the other side of the church, this one in a rose-colored garment.

The artist had posed this one as though it were swooping down from heaven. The feet were straight up in the air, and the hair streamed behind as though caught by the wind. It was bent at the waist with the head tilted up and the trumpet pointed at a rakish angle. I saw a certain freedom in the pose. While the first angel presumably played, "Glory to God," I thought I could hear this one playing, "Toot, toot, Whoopee!" or perhaps a bar or two of Oscar Peterson or John Coltrane.

Both angels touched a chord deep within me, and each carried the right message for me for the time it appeared. Over the past year I had been given a new sense of freedom. I had experienced the exhilaration of flying, of walking through life without touching the ground. And it had come as I realized that God would do the work of changing me and making me what we both wanted *if I would let him*. He would make the most amazing changes, helping me do those things I ought to do and not do the things I ought not to do. He didn't expect me to fly on my own. I didn't have to tough it out to keep the commandments, to follow a set of rules by sheer determination. I didn't have to beat back the temptation to be, let's say, rude or vain or insensitive or lazy. God would do it if I would wait on him.

It is a subtle but critical truth. Andrew Murray, in *Waiting on God*, put it like this: "God cannot part with His grace or goodness or strength as an external thing that He gives us, as He gives the raindrops from heaven. No, He can only give it, and we can enjoy it, as He works it Himself directly and unceasingly." This is what the Scripture means when it says that it is God who works in us to will and to do his good pleasure (Phil. 2:13). And the paradox is that in this declaration of dependence, we find freedom.

Having learned this sustaining truth, I also realize I continually block it out. I approach problems and events as though I have no recourse but my own will to summon the wisdom or peace or love or patience or kindness or whatever virtue is necessary at the time. In effect I declare my independence.

When my son Todd graduated from high school, his class of nineteen pointed a few last-minute gibes at the adult world they were about to enter. Resplendent in white evening clothes, they sat in a row facing proud parents, high on a Virginia hillside in front of the old mansion that was their school. I still have the clipping with the photo from the newspaper. They look like any other group of high school students—dressed and smiling for the great occasion—except for one thing: they have no shoes on.

I thought of it as their declaration of independence. For the occasion Todd had written a parody of Frank Sinatra's "I Did It My Way." That, too, I thought of as his way of saying, "I worked hard for this, and I'm proud of it." I know how he felt. I've experienced that same pride of accomplishment in a job well done—

in a piece of writing or a project completed, for example, or a part in a team effort.

Nevertheless I've come to think of those words "I Did It My Way" as a concise expression of our universal determination to usurp the place of God. Adam's essential sin was to do what he wanted to do, not what God wanted, and in so doing he replaced God in his life with his own will. Despite the overwhelming evidence and the years of experience that tell me the God who created the universe loves me and wants me to follow him, and despite my understanding of the consequences to the contrary, I persist in trying to do it my way. I know from long, sad experience that I don't do the things I know I should do and that I want to do. And I do a lot of things I wish I hadn't. So if the whim of those high schoolers so many years ago was a small declaration of independence, I fully understand it.

This is where the search for the sacrament of the present moment comes to bear and where the excitement of finding it comes in. Faced with a situation or event, a problem or need, we wait on God to see what he will do, how he will direct, what means he'll use to accomplish his will. Actively aware that he is working, we wait to see the result.

I don't mean to leave the impression that God requires nothing of us. Letting God work is not a spectator sport in which we sit on the sidelines cheering

God on. God requires both discipline and self-control. But it is God who gives them. Holding on to God and to the awareness of him, seeking to be heavenly minded while living on earth, constantly looking into every crack and corner and cupboard of life, expecting to see him because he is there, requires the discipline that only God can give. But the great secret is, in that alone is freedom.

The angels have returned each year a few weeks before Christmas, and even as I write they hang larger than life, seeming to frolic, on the wall at the front of the church. They remind me of a less happier time of my life, of course, but more than that they remind me of how, as I came to God in a helpless heap, he turned my life upside down and around and did amazing things I never could have imagined.

I received a call recently from a friend, a recovering addict who is normally compulsive, wanting all problems to be solved and decisions to be made immediately, if not sooner. He is in a painful and complicated passage of life, and I heard him acknowledge that it might take months or years to resolve this one and to heal all wounds. It was understanding, I believe, straight from God. It was a result of God working his will in this man's life, teaching him—and reminding me—that *letting God work* in our lives is not an instant, one-time event.

So I welcome the angels. They come at an appropriate time of year, not just on the anniversary of a traumatic event in my life, but just before the beginning of the New Year. I don't know how long is the pilgrimage ahead, but I know one of the most uplifting truths of the Christian life is that at any time, we can put the past behind and begin a new stage of the journey.

The Long Journey

It took me thirty hours and four flights to return from Singapore to Virginia, exactly halfway around the earth. It was the longest trip I'd ever made without stopping overnight, and I was exhausted long before I reached home.

Still, compared to travel before the age of steam or combustion, it was but a flash. We don't really know what long journeys are today. It took Hudson Taylor six months the first time he sailed from England to China. Lewis and Clark trekked for eighteen months to cross the American frontier and back. A routine trip from Washington to Philadelphia in 1800 took several days, not several hours. Today, overnight bags have replaced steamer trunks. We jet halfway across the country for a business lunch and return in time for dinner. Perhaps that's why we fail to appreciate the Christian life as a pilgrimage. There are no weekend excursions to the Promised Land.

Eugene Peterson (quoting Friedrich Nietzsche) called for "a long obedience in the same direction." This world is not our home, so we set out for our Father's house. Some clever engineer once figured out how to put a clock in my computer, so now I can call up each of the stories and reflections I have written here and see the exact date and time I wrote them or last worked on them. They did not, however, happen in an instant. They are not sudden revelations for which I can pinpoint the place or the occasion on the journey at which God spoke. I can't put them in chronological order. I think of them as growing insights from God into the poverty of my own spiritual condition reflected in the mirror of his holiness. The closer I draw to the mirror, the clearer the reflection becomes. I am on a long journey in the direction of that holiness, and as Peterson indicated, God calls for continual obedience.

I've recorded a few more of these insights here. I had a lot to learn about pain, for example, and in the process I learned to cry. At the same time I needed to move away from the continuous introspection into which I had fallen. I had to leave the holy huddle and make contact with some who had more pressing needs than mine. And then, as I sought the fruit of patience, I learned how closely related it is to pride. I hope that the telling will make your load lighter and your pilgrimage more fruitful as you move down the road in the direction of heaven.

To Live Is to Dance

Watching God Work through the Pain

> Keep on doing what we told you to do to please God, not in a dogged religious plod, but in a living, spirited dance.
>
> *1 Thessalonians 4:1* TM

My father loved to dance. He had one of those old, windup Victrolas and a stack of scratchy 78s of Les Brown, Kay Kaiser, Woody Herman and the other big bands of the thirties and forties. Put on a record, and he couldn't sit still. He'd shuffle his feet and move around the room, his feet and arms and body translating what he felt inside. He danced with my mother; he danced with my sister; he taught me to dance. He picked up his grandchildren when they were small and danced with them in his arms. Shortly before he died, he and my mother were still whirling around the dance floor.

So I guess the urge comes naturally for me. All my life I had wanted to tap dance, so when I was single again and able to follow the fancy, I tacked a pair of taps onto black dancing shoes and went to class. “Hop, shuffle, step, fa-lap; hop, shuffle, step, fa-lap!” I was at least twice the age of anyone else in the class and had a little trouble matching the coordination of the kids, but I loved it. I practiced faithfully an hour a day, learned the Irish, the Cincinnati, the Buffalo, the Hollywood Double Buck Time Step, and watched videos of the best hoofers tappin’ today, like Gregory Hines, Tommy Tune, Brenda Buffalino, and Sandman Sims.

I’ve hung up my taps now. That fling is over. But dancing has become for me, as it often is in literature, a metaphor of life. The movements of the dance depict the passages, the rituals, the sentiments, the very story of life-birth, growing up, conflict, loneliness, mating, death, and the rest. Dance can, if we allow it, express base instincts. If we let the flesh rule while we dance, it can be little more than lust. If we seek simply to satisfy our own fancy and follow our own aspirations, the dance degenerates into a meaningless set of motions. But walk through life with an awareness of the Spirit, and we can express the highest degree of ecstasy in God by moving our feet, arms, and body.

Southern storyteller Terry Kay has written a tale about an elderly man grieving for his wife of fifty-seven years. In his loneliness Sam Peek befriends a stray, white dog who in one scene puts his paws on Sam's walker. When Sam moves the walker back, the dog moves with him. When Sam moves to the side, the dog follows. "I'll be damned," says the old man. "First time I ever danced with a dog."

Kay took the title of the book *To Dance with the White Dog* from this scene. The dog becomes the man's companion, and on his death bed Sam tells his family he believes the white dog was his wife, Cora, come back to watch over him. The story is "a loving eulogy to old age," one critic wrote, and the dance, mentioned only once in the book, stuck in my mind as a symbol of the last struggles of one old man.

Dance as a metaphor of life is right out of the Scriptures. While Moses was on the mountain, the Israelites made a calf out of gold, had a great feast, got drunk, and danced. They got up to indulge in revelry, the Bible says, but not to honor God.

On the other hand, King David was so thrilled to have the ark of the covenant back in Jerusalem that he danced with all his might. It was his way of expressing his joy and honoring God at the same time. "Praise him with tambourine and dancing," the psalmist writes (Ps. 150:4). And when the prodigal son returned, the father gave a feast, and the guests danced to express their joy in the return of one who had been lost. There is "a time to weep and a time to laugh, a time to mourn and a time to dance," writes the Teacher, in the book of Ecclesiastes (3:4).

While dance may be a metaphor of life, it strikes me as an odd one. We usually associate dancing with happy times. We dance at weddings and graduations and other celebrations. So what about the times of sorrow? Actually, says Henri Nouwen, the time to mourn and the time to dance may be the same. "The dance does not simply *follow* the grief," he writes, "it finds its origin in the grieving itself" *(The New Oxford Review)*. So it was appropriate, perhaps, that I took up tap dancing in the midst of the most wrenching pain I have ever felt. Prostrate through a staggering loss, I looked up and found I was alive. With little to lose I took the first small steps on shaky legs and found that life was worth dancing. In acknowledging that my pain was a part of life, and not attempting to *tough* it out, I was able to let others minister to me in a way that allowed the healing to begin.

I haven't always done that. Conditioned by a culture that considers crying a feminine response to deep emotion and not appropriate for men, I had not shed many tears since childhood. I subscribed to the adage "When the going gets tough, the tough get going." I got on with life and admitted no pain to myself, much less to anyone else. But during this period of grief, God opened my tear ducts and the flood came forth. I learned that I could not only cry but I could get angry and scream, and it was okay. God loved me. Tears, I learned, are neither masculine nor feminine. They are a human response to suffering.

Today a tender scene in a book or film or a poignant moment with a friend or even a time of reflection before God brings tears quickly. My eyes fill up and I have to catch my breath before I can speak. I'm glad for this. I think it's healthy and I find it satisfying to let the emotion flow out with the tears. Tears are only the outward indication that I'm able to feel the pain—my own and others—and that I'm not denying the experience of it.

I think it's important now that I continue to mourn and cry as well as to dance and celebrate, and to share both with those who care. It's important that I don't deny the daily losses of life we all experience. About eight years ago while fishing, a small, lead jig snapped back and smashed into my right eye, and I lost forever some of the sight in that eye and my depth perception.

(During the operation to reattach the retina, I asked the surgeon if I'd be able to play a good game of tennis after he took the bandage off. "Sure," he said. "That's wonderful," I told him, "because I never could play before.")

I have a friend who lives on the West Coast, 3,000 miles away from me, too far to visit and enjoy his company regularly. Once we lived in the same neighborhood, but then I was too afraid to let him close, to expose my weaknesses and share my pain. I've cried for that and for other opportunities lost, dreams dissolved, time wasted. And as I have shared the pain of each of these, I have found, as Nouwen puts it, the beginning movements of the dance.

I have a new dance partner now. Give Mary half a chance, and she's ready to whirl. We danced at our wedding, and on occasion we dance between the kitchen and the living room. On a trip to New Orleans we visited a dance hall where a Cajun band played for local folks and a few stray tourists. Cajun dancing is done to a two-step with formal routines like the jitterbug of the fifties. We stood at the edge of the crowded dance floor and admired the skill of various couples, wishing we had learned the steps but afraid we'd embarrass ourselves if we tried.

Suddenly a man approached Mary and asked her to dance. "I don't know how," she shrugged, thinking that would discourage him. "Can you count to two?" he smiled. She had time only to nod before he reached for her hand and pulled her onto the floor. For the next four or five minutes he skillfully guided her through the various routines of Cajun dancing, and I watched as the anxiety on her face turned to pure enjoyment.

Is there another metaphor in that? Anxiety dissolving into joy, sadness emerging into celebration, grief generating a lively dance? Perhaps! I visited a church once that experimented with liturgy. The pastor wore a stole, and on each side was an embroidered cartoon of Snoopy the dog, dancing. On one side an inscription read, “To dance is to live,” and on the other side, “To live is to dance.” I love it! I’ll grieve again, I’m sure. But I’m just as sure that I’ll arise from my loss and begin a spirited, foot-tapping, arm-swinging, body-moving dance of life.

Out of the Holy Huddle

Beyond Introspection

I drive a pickup, a 1990 Mazda B2200 with a king cab, rear seats, and bed liner. I bought it, I told myself, because my twelve-foot fishing boat fits neatly into the back, and when you live in the country, you need a truck. In four years I've carried a dozen loads of horse manure, a piano, farm machinery, firewood, and all manner of furniture. A friend once borrowed it to cart several port-a-potties to rural homes without indoor plumbing.

In a way I never anticipated, however, my pickup has often been my link to the community, the means by which I've reached out a little beyond my comfortable Christian clutch and made some contact with people who have much more pressing needs. Mostly I've done small errands I could easily squeeze into my flexible schedule, like moving a sofa, chairs, and a table for a single mother, or driving an AIDS patient to the clinic. On several occasions I went fishing with a young man who had a brain tumor. I was going fishing anyhow, so it was no problem for me to put John in the front seat and put a fishing pole in his hands. Like me, he didn't really care much if he caught anything. He just enjoyed riding around the lake on a sunny day.

These were minor acts of loving my neighbor, enough to produce a sense of wanting to do more, if not guilt for how little I do. I live in a community in which it's too easy to go from home to church to the office to the mall and back without ever noticing hardscrabble poverty or people with acute physical needs. But they're there. And a faint but annoying voice, like an itch that's hard to get at, tells me that I should be too.

"The goal of authentic spirituality," writes theologian Richard Lovelace, "is a love which escapes from the closed circle of spiritual self-indulgence, or even self-improvement, to become absorbed in the love of God and other persons." Holiness should produce service. True faith will be followed by works. All the religious exercises and speech and profession of love in the world mean nothing if they don't result in action. It isn't an either/or. The twin commands—love the Lord with all your heart, and love your neighbor as yourself—sum up the balanced Christian life.

The weight of what I have been writing about in this book is on the formation of the inner life. I have been in a back-to-the-basics-of-Christianity mode, a kind of Spiritual Calisthenics 101 class, in which I've reviewed the fundamentals of the faith, such as acknowledging the depth of my sin, waiting on God, dealing with pride, etc. I've been back to boot camp, to switch metaphors, where I've had a refresher course in the weapons of spiritual warfare. Or to raise still another image, I have been refitted with spiritual bifocals to help me look inward, as well as beyond the end of my nose. Now the time has come for me to use the top part of these spectacles and focus a little more on the landscape of service.

So I've been reassessing my gifts, abilities, time, and experience. I mentioned earlier that I often ask myself what it is that I really like to do. I believe the Lord often plants the desire in us because he wants us to do a particular task for him. But that kind of reasoning has a few caveats. For one thing, a job for which we're qualified and called may have some tasks attached to it that we find difficult or tedious or stressful.

Committees are my affliction. I marvel at the skill with which some people work in committee meetings. Personally I like the old saying that a committee should be made up of no more than three people, two of them absent. Committees are fallen structures run by fallen people and can activate latent egos. It requires humility as well as wisdom to work in committees. More committee meetings should begin with foot-washing ceremonies, as well as prayer. This may be why I'm on more committees now than I've ever been in my life. There I may learn some of the pitfalls of pride and the submission of service that God wants me to learn.

Then again, we sometimes use service to justify our neglect of some other responsibilities, for example, our families. Service begins at home. If we don't serve in little ways the people we love best, we may question our motivation for serving those we don't know as well. Service means putting ourselves below someone else, and it's harder to do that with those we know best. I have marveled many times at Mary's commitment to serve her children and me and her willingness to put her family before her own comfort, convenience, and out-of-the-home career. We can't serve our family when we're not home. I don't believe God calls us to frenzied living. If we're scooting from one meeting or commitment to another, out nine nights a week, getting reacquainted with our families as we pass through the house, then either we have not learned to say no to the demands, or we're not responding to them in a healthy fashion.

It also takes a lot of walking among the rows of our reasoning to spot the weeds of self-deceit. Why are we drawn toward certain types of service? Why would I rather sit beside a hospital bed than sit in a committee meeting? Or write a piece for the church newsletter rather than teach a Sunday school class? Besides examining our gifts we have to examine our motivations. Richard Foster says that much service is "self-righteous service." It's done for mixed motivations.

The pilgrimage of my friend Bob Osborne illustrates well the difference between service done for self and service that grows out of a profound love of Christ. As a college freshman in the sixties, he was moved by the experience and simple lifestyle of an early Peace Corps worker. It all sounded so good and right. So Bob signed up right after college, and for the next ten years rose through the ranks of government and private development agencies with stints in Uganda, Mozambique, and Kenya.

"I was idealistic," he remembers. "I thought the answer to poverty was the redistribution of resources. I was driven by causes. I was caught up in the program of trying to help the poor through better programs."

Isolated in a small expatriate community in Mozambique, Bob and his wife, Nancy, whom he met when she was a Peace Corps worker, became friends with a Mennonite couple who broke the mold of relief and development workers. "It was obvious," Bob recalls, "that Christ was part of everything in their lives." And it was the beginning of a serious Christian commitment for both Bob and Nancy.

As Bob's faith grew, his values and motivations changed. "Like most relief and development types, I was motivated by approval and the perks that followed—the big car and home and the benefit package." So when both Bob and the agency he worked for realized their goals were different, shaped by dissimilar values, they both knew the time for separation had come.

"Still," Bob says, "it took awhile for me to realize that God wants to be at the center of my work for the poor, rather than the poor being at the center. We need to be about the business of reconciliation. That's what moves me, the recognition that God saw me in my need and reconciled me to him. He didn't put any conditions on it. He just loved me as I am. And I want that to characterize my work with the poor." To reach the poor today Bob directs a local agency that coordinates the outreach of many churches.

The question of what form my service will take is a minor one. There is no lack of opportunities, and God has a way of putting them in front of me until I bump my nose on them. I am more concerned with several other questions that I'll always need to ask.

First, what are my motivations? Why do I want to take on this job? For self-righteous reasons or out of response to the love of Christ for me? And secondly, is my love for Christ, in response to his unconditional love for me, so fervent that it will continually move me to demonstrate that love, whatever the risk or discomfort?

Grow Old Along with Me

Watching God Work in Old Age

I had slipped into the fast food restaurant between early morning appointments, hoping for a few minutes to clear my head and get ready for my next meeting. So I took my coffee and roll to a table near a window with no one close by. Some thirty feet away, however, some old men had set up camp, nursing coffee from styrofoam cups and pronouncing judgment on local and world events. The one who had the most to say had the loudest voice, and he advised everyone without a hearing deficiency of his opinions on highway construction, hardshell Baptists, getting drunk on Friday night, and a few other topics.

In the thirty minutes I sat there, I watched the group change. Some left while others came, but the outspoken one remained, a kind of anchorman for the morning meeting of the local association of retirees.

I suppose this scene is played out daily in coffee shops across the country. Hair white and thinning, hands gnarled, liver spots covering wrinkled skin, their raised voices betraying their own hearing handicap, they pass the hours in conversation, sifting through the past, retelling old stories, speculating on life as it struts before them.

I'm a long way from that stage, but as I listened unintentionally, I recalled a comment my daughter Heather had made years ago. We had just moved from a suburb of Chicago to a hamlet in Virginia, and she was not at all thrilled with the idea. One day as we drove past a group of men sitting idly on the stoop of a country store, she muttered, "There's Dad!" I was only forty-six at the time, so I could afford to be amused. But watching those old men in the coffee shop raised images of my grandfathers. I was about ten years old when they were in their early sixties. My mother's father, as I recall him, was a rascal, a short, tough working man who liked to tease me and always smelled of beer. I liked him. My father's father was a stern-faced product of an Ivy League school who worked for a blue chip company all his life and sat around in a shirt and tie at all hours of the day. I disturbed him at my own risk, but more often I tiptoed around him. As far as I was concerned at the time, the two grandfathers had only one thing in common: they were both old. At that age, I thought, you had a past but not much to look forward to. I thought senior citizens had little to do except rock. Shaped by a culture that measures human worth in terms of production, I saw the old and retired as relics on a shelf, with primarily a decorative function and an occasional assignment to entertain small children.

Now I see things differently. I've learned our value lies not in the number of words we write, nor in the number of people we serve, nor the wealth we create. Knowing and loving God and becoming like him is the object of it all, and God is no respecter of age. I have my work cut out for me for whatever number of days or years God grants me.

Part of seeing God work is the recognition that his work in us is a process, not an achievement. By that I mean we do not, once for all, attain a quality or a virtue never to lose it. Once we believe we've arrived, we are back to square one. It is Satan, not the Spirit of God, who whispers, "See how you've grown. Look how you've become like Jesus."

We don't suddenly, through grace, become loving, patient, generous, sensitive, or wise. We become these momentarily, over and over again. We are these at any given instant. They are not possessions. They are not integral to our being in a way that without them we are not ourselves. They are only expressions of a state of being, isolated applications of various teachings. We are loving, patient, generous, sensitive, or wise in any one act.

The process of watching for God to work puts a new spin on life, no matter what age. It adds excitement, a sense of expectancy. What wonderful thing will God do next? I can hardly wait. Perhaps this is what David in Psalm 51 referred to as "the joy of your salvation." More and more I anticipate something good to happen, and I enjoy it more when it does.

I can't really see myself as part of the styrofoam-clutching coffee crowd at the nearest fast food restaurant. I have full use of my faculties, plus honest employment, and I'm finding more enjoyment and fulfillment in life than I ever have. Actually I have rarely lacked in my life for "something to do." I've always had more interests to pursue than time and energy would permit. My to-do list is unmanageable. I have a half dozen books in the "read soon" category. Before I leave on my next trip, I'd like to learn a little conversational Chinese. I'm thinking about building a darkroom this summer, and I want to study more about computers. On occasion I wish I could get back to my tap dancing, and I have an old boat I want to clean up and get in the water. And all these fall second to several church programs I'm involved in. Yet in this new spiritual passage, I'm finding more reward in anticipating what God will do and in watching him as he does it than in any of the above.

I like the way Eugene Peterson has expressed this idea in his paraphrase of Paul's letter to the Romans. "The created world itself can hardly wait for what's coming next. Everything in creation is being more or less held back. God reins it in until both creation and all the creatures are ready and can be released at the same moment into the glorious times ahead. Meanwhile the joyful anticipation deepens."

The more I see God work in my own life, the more I believe he will continue. Like a pregnant woman, I grow larger in expectancy. Meanwhile I keep in mind the opening line of Scott Peck's *The Road Less Traveled:* "Life is difficult." But more and more I see these difficulties as birth pangs, as pain that will lead to a wonderful deliverance some day ahead. Shortly after the passage in which he writes about holy expectancy, Paul reminds the Romans that none of the pains, no matter how severe, can separate us from the love of God.

I have sufficient experience now in the spiritual life to say with confidence that as long as I am watching I will see "the footprints of the Holy" in the sands of my life. "Everything that happens each moment bears the stamp of God's will," de Caussade writes. "Those who have abandoned themselves to God always lead mysterious lives and receive from him exceptional and miraculous gifts by means of the most ordinary, natural and chance experiences in which there appears to be nothing unusual. The simplest sermon, the most banal conversations, the least erudite books become a source of knowledge and wisdom to these souls by virtue of God's purpose. This is why they carefully pick up the crumbs which clever minds tread under foot, for to them everything is precious and a source of enrichment" *(Sacrament)*.

It seems to me that what de Caussade and Thomas Kelly and Brother Lawrence are talking about is filling all the holes in life with God. Finding the sacrament of each moment means not letting big gaps of Godless time appear in our lives, not neglecting the awareness of and communion with God for hours or even minutes on end.

I've walked only a few steps down the road of this awesome and profound style of living. My life, in practice, is more a division between my time and God time. But I'm committed to blending the sacred and the secular and letting God intrude more and more into each point of my life.

My New Year's Resolution

The Humility I Haven't Achieved

I always thought of my Aunt Elsie as an eccentric old lady (although at the time I remember her, she wasn't all that old). She never married, and she doted on my two brothers and sister and me. On Sunday afternoons and holidays we often went to my grandfather's house where she gave us lavish parties or taught us to play bridge or drilled us in table manners and etiquette.

"Don't spoon your coffee out of a cup like soup."

"When you eat soup, tilt the bowl away from you."

"Don't begin to eat until everyone is served."

"When someone pays you a compliment, say, 'Thank you.'"

Elsie had many fixations, which served as moorings and lent a form of permanence to her life. She had a favorite color—green—and insisted we have one as well. She loved pansies, and we could be sure she'd like her Christmas gift if we chose one with pansies on it. Elsie also believed firmly in New Year's resolutions, and every New Year's Day, after the big dining room table was cleared, she sat us down with pencil and paper and made us compose ten resolutions. Fortunately she did not insist on seeing them.

I smile now at her odd habits, but I have practiced that last one ever since. I don't insist on ten of them, but for most of my life on New Year's Day I have written down or stuffed into the back of my head some serious resolutions for improving my life in the coming year. This year I have resolved to let the fruit of patience grow in my life.

Patience is the fourth—and much-neglected—fruit of the Spirit mentioned in Galatians 5:22–23. We talk a lot about the first three—love, joy, peace—but not so much about this very important quality. "True patience," Andrew Murray wrote, "is the losing of our self-will in His perfect will." It takes a great depth of humility to get to the point where we're truly afraid to exercise our own will because we're sure we'll mess things up. And I suspect it was in recognizing this lack of humility that I made the resolution. Pride, the opposite of humility, is the curse that plagues me and robs me of patience.

It is, in fact, just when I think I've achieved some extra measure of patience with people and events that I lose it. Pride sticks its ugly nose under the corner of the tent and soon upends the furniture of my life.

Impatience is the handmaiden of pride and leads to self-justification and self-righteousness. I am impatient, for example, with what I perceive to be incompetence. Oh, I don't mind waiting in long checkout lines at the supermarket. I realize that God is using this test to develop patience in me. But why is that checker so slow? And why doesn't the management provide someone to bag the groceries? Am I supposed to stand around here while they try to get their act together? I've got things to do. I've got to get home and finish this chapter on patience.

Like everyone else in our Western work world, I have a to-do list, which I keep on my computer. Actually it's a list of lists with projects for my clients, correspondence, phone calls, errands, jobs around the house. I carefully maintain the list, add new tasks under the appropriate headings, and get a great feeling of accomplishment as I delete jobs I've done. This master list is intended to relieve my mind, assuring me I haven't forgotten anything. I've got it all under control. I just have to look at the list. Of course, that's part of the problem. The list is so long that one glance at it could raise my anxiety level several notches, and every interruption of my plans easily becomes an irritation.

For years I bought into the modern myth that I could add endlessly to the list with just a little better organization. Technology will make me more efficient;

management methods will make me more effective. Get up an hour earlier; work while I eat lunch; take a course in speed reading; listen to tapes while I drive.

Several years ago I reasoned away the myth. It's a foolish and destructive illusion. I'm mortal, with obvious and increasing limitations.

Next I told myself that if I used my time well, followed the Spirit in what I did, and still didn't get everything done that I had planned that day, God knew it. I simply hadn't planned well. When interruptions came, I could handle them. I'd know that God is in control, so I'd not be impatient with the friend or even the salesperson who wanted to talk. I'd wait in bumper-to-bumper traffic with perfect equanimity, even using the time to pray.

I knew even before I read Thomas Kelly's *A Testament of Devotion* that the problem was not having too much to do, but my response to it. Kelly argues skillfully that we blame the complexity of our lives on the complex nature of our society. "We Western people are apt to think our great problems are external, environmental," he writes. "We are not skilled in the inner life, where the real roots of our problem lie. For I would suggest that the true explanation of the complexity of our program is an inner one, not an outer one." Still, it was an intellectual argument, all in my head. And it didn't produce a lot of change in my response to external pressures.

In recent days, however, I've noticed a small change. As I've become more and more aware of the presence of God throughout my waking hours, no matter what task I'm engaged in, and as I've spent more time in wordless communion with him, I have felt less hurried, more apt to see the interruptions as part of God's plan, more content to sit in the traffic, less upset when I reschedule uncompleted projects. "If we *center down*," Kelly writes, using an old Quaker phrase, "and live in that holy Silence that is dearer than life, and take our life program into the silent places of the heart, with complete openness, ready to do, ready to renounce according to His leading, then many of the things we are doing lose their vitality for us."

This resolution to let the fruit of patience grow in my life has many implications. Developing patience, by definition, requires distress, to put it mildly. Patience is the act of bearing adversity calmly. Patience doesn't grow in a vacuum nor in the garden of good fortune. It comes only under constraint and is fertilized by suffering. So I'll not be surprised when adversity comes.

I'm also learning that my patience may be a balm for healing in the lives of others. Life is a series of losses that need healing, and my patience with those who are grappling with their losses aids their healing. In letting them be angry, for example, I acknowledge their wounds and help the healing to take place. I accept their woundedness because I know I have my own wounds and losses to deal with. As I am wounded and scarred in my daily encounter with life—even if I get only a few scratches and bruises—I need the healing ointment that can be applied by someone else's patient care. I want to perform that healing role in the life of my family as a beginning. But I realize I may also play it in small ways in the lives of many others and never know it.

I think it would be a great compliment to have someone say, "He is a very patient man." Greater still would it be to have my family say that. Today as I write, we are completing two weeks of exceptionally cold weather. Below-zero temperatures, snow, ice, and freezing rain have caused school to be canceled and confined us to the house with only occasional forays for groceries. We have consumed books, puzzles, board games, and videos. And while it can't be classed as a great hardship, the experience has called for unusual flexibility and tested the patience of all. This came, as you might expect, as a prelude to writing this chapter, and it conveniently followed my resolve to let the Spirit grow patience in me.

The very process I have been writing about, that of watching God work in our lives, requires patience. "The entire resignation of the will that only wants to be a vessel in which His holy will can move and mold is not found at once," says Murray in *Waiting on God*.

Growth doesn't come with the snap of the fingers. God doesn't pour in water and mix to get instant perfection in us. I need to be patient with God, even while he works patience in me. That may be more difficult in a society that has made instant gratification an art form, but the process of sanctification will go on for the rest of my life. This doesn't excuse impatience; it simply recognizes a natural process of life.

The by-product of patience is hope. "I waited patiently for the Lord," David the psalmist writes, and "he put a new song in my mouth" (Ps. 40:1, 3). I could use a little new music. I don't always like the tunes I play. I'd be pleased if God would write a new melody and the words to go with it and let me sing it. Something upbeat, Lord. Something I can dance to, perhaps. And Lord, please hurry!

The Problem of Not Understanding

God Works in Wondrous Ways

I enjoy a good spy book, but it's hard to find one that's well written, one in which the characters have depth, the prose is clean, and the plot skillfully developed. Most of them are potboilers turned out by word mechanics who have found a successful formula that includes a lot of violence and some gratuitous sex. When I find a good one, however, I lose myself in it while the world goes its way.

I've learned something helpful from these books, however: A good spymaster tells an agent only what he needs to know. There is a master plan for the operation, but each agent, partly for his protection, sees only his part and not the whole. So it is with God. As I watch him work in my small world, I realize that he reveals to me only an infinitesimal part of his plan for creation, only what I need to know—and when I need to know it.

This often requires a lot of faith. In the midst of crushing loss, defeat, or failure, when bad things happen to good people, when good things happen to bad people, when life at face value makes no sense at all, it requires of us a deep conviction of God's love, his complete control, and his master plan.

So it was as Mary and I looked at a dream we had dared to nourish. Some months before we had sat in slightly padded but straight-backed chairs across the desk from a social worker. She was well cast for the job, professional yet with a slightly matronly manner. The office itself was small, the furnishings comfortable, the decor not memorable. We had come to pursue the glimmer of a wild idea that we had mentioned to only a few close friends—we wanted to adopt an older child.

Mary had first voiced the idea. She had begun to ask aloud what she'd do when Clint, ten at the time, needed less and less of her attention. "I'm a nurturer," she had often told me, and in turn I had complimented her on her parenting skills and on her down-home gift of common sense. We had the will, the energy, the resources, and the experience—so why not?

Cautiously, then, we had come to this office to explore the idea, and when the caseworker slid a harmless-looking, yellow notebook across the desk to us, we unknowingly opened it. It was the so-called ARIVA book—Adoption Resources in Virginia. Each page in the three-ring binder held a colored photo and a description of a child available for adoption. They were anywhere from two to fourteen years old, and many had problems such as a learning disability or cerebral palsy or a cleft palate.

But as I began to turn the pages, I realized that these cherubic faces were not just available. They were waiting, beckoning, silently crying for someone to claim them as their own. Each was a refugee from a domestic disaster—an unwed mother, an abusive father, parents who abandoned them. With a shudder I closed the book and handed it back to the social worker. We weren't shopping. If God had a child for us, we weren't going to pick it out of a catalog like an appliance or a ski vacation. This woman wanted only to open our eyes to what we could expect, not to have us choose. But I wanted to take them all. I wanted to gather them from wherever they were languishing and give them what every child needs: a loving home.

In the next few months the agency completed an intensive examination of our lives and our home. They probed our relationship and our views on parenting. They delved into our family history. "Any record of mental illness, substance abuse, criminal convictions?" they asked. What did our grown children think of the idea? How were our finances? And our health? Satisfied that we could handle the task, they pronounced us satisfactory and began the search for the right child.

The idea that I again might parent a small child after a hiatus of many years had come as a surprise. Sarah laughed when God told Abraham they'd have a child in their old age, and while I'm hardly Abrahamic, most of my contemporaries pack pictures of grandchildren in their wallets. But it didn't surprise me that God likes to surprise us. We like to surprise people, and he made us in his image. Salvation itself came as a surprise to me. God's love, God's will, God's way of working in this world often surprises me.

A bigger surprise awaited us. Shortly after the agency put their stamp of approval on us as certified parents for adoption, Mary suddenly began to deal with some unresolved incidents in her own childhood. For the next year she needed all her emotional energy to deal with intense anxieties, and it became apparent to us we had to put the dream on a shelf. All God's surprises aren't as pleasant as others.

Dietrich Bonhoeffer wrote to his fiancée from prison about "man's confusion at God's providence." Why at age thirty-nine did God lead him to the love of his life, just as the Nazis locked him up in prison? Bonhoeffer speculated and wrote his conclusion to Maria von Wedemeyer, "I believe that our union can only be a sign of God's grace and kindness, which calls us to faith."

I can't make any more sense out of it than that. Why did God lead Mary and me through that long process of inquiring into the adoption of a child? The excitement had grown as we thought about a little person entering our lives and our home. An older child would probably have severe problems of one kind or another, emotional or physical or both. So we prayed for grace and understanding. In the end we needed both, but not the way we expected.

I think Bonhoeffer had the key to it. While God's providence (which we don't always recognize as such) may surprise, startle, overwhelm, or confuse us, it should in the long run call us to faith. It should point us to him.

Each of us has experienced traumatic loss or disappointment or puzzling circumstances we can't understand. Why did God let my parents abandon me? Why did my child die at birth? What is God trying to tell me? Why did he lead me so far only to snatch it all away? Why? Is there any meaning in it all?

I've not spent a lot of time in my life agonizing over *why*. The question is always there, beneath the surface like the 90 percent of the iceberg. Even if we don't cry out in anger or pout or turn away from God, we can't escape it. But I've come to accept that there are many things in life I'll never understand and some that I wouldn't understand even if someone explained them. I once attended a lecture for lay people on the human immunodeficiency virus, which is the cause of AIDS. The lecturer, a physician, tried his best to make hematology, the branch of biology that deals with blood, understandable to people like me who had majored in the humanities. He lost me in the first five minutes, and I spent the rest of the hour trying to look interested and intelligent.

More importantly, however, I have not spent a lot of time over the years asking why God allows these things to happen *because I know why:* to change me, to make me like himself. Suffering produces perseverance, Paul writes in Romans 5:3–4, and perseverance brings out character and character leads to hope. That is not to say that God goes around inflicting pain on people whom he decides he'd like to refine more than others. Several years ago in the midst of my grief a good friend suggested that God must have something special in mind for me if he would bring such loss into my life.

Does that mean, I wondered, that God does not have something special in mind for those not called to suffer in the same way? No! Trials of all kinds should deepen our faith, as gold is purified by fire. But the operative word here is *allow*. God allows them to happen, and grace carries us through them. But pain, ultimately, is the result of evil. And God hates evil. Period!

A number of books offer biblical and logical explanations for the problem of pain. If God is good, and if he is all-powerful, why does he allow bad things to happen to those he loves? It's good for us to grapple with these questions and to understand the doctrines of the fall and of evil, which in turn help us understand the problem of pain. It's reassuring to know that it all makes sense, that suffering does not stem from the whims of a capricious God. But in the midst of grief and heartache, it is generally not the intellectual understanding of evil that brings relief. For many—I suspect, for most—Christians who could not write a simple explanation of suffering for an exam, it is the assurance of God's love imparted by the Spirit that carries them through. The rational grasp of why there is suffering does augment hope. But it is personal acquaintance and familiarity with God himself that brings comfort.

Sadly, it often takes times of intense pain or confusion to drive us into the presence of God. We blunder along with nodding acquiescence toward God in our lives until we're desperate. Then we get serious about our relationship and seek his comfort, for a time. The kind of living that I've been talking about, in which God is never far from our consciousness, is not insurance against pain. It doesn't make grief any less. But it does give us a sense of peace in the midst of the pain. It equips us to bear it, to endure with the assurance of experience that God is there. If we have developed this habit of living out of the Divine Center, as Thomas Kelly calls it, of letting our responses to life be regulated by the Presence who is never far from us, it also carries us through the times of turmoil.

God's sense of timing is often far beyond our understanding. Several years ago I had contracts for enough editorial work to consume half my time, and I had committed the other half of my time to writing a book. I didn't have a contract for the book, however, so it was a risk.

I had sought the advice of friends. I believed that the book I wanted to write would honor God. Still, I had responsibilities, a mortgage to pay, a family to feed. Was I reading God's instructions right? Or had I read some of my own will into them?

To answer that last question, I reflected on my childhood. I inherited my love of books. My mother, a reluctant housekeeper, would often prop up a book in front of her at the kitchen sink while she washed dishes. I recall frequent family trips to the library before I could go by myself, and it was common in my house to see four or five of us sitting around a Saturday lunch table, each with our nose stuck in a book and a sandwich stuck in our mouth. Somehow I acquired this idea that everything I need to know is written in a book. And I still find more enjoyment in sitting in bed, propped up with pillows, a plate of crackers and cheese at my elbow and a good book in hand, than almost anything else.

Before I set out to write this particular book, I applied a three-way test to know God's will: Do I have the desire? Do I have the ability? Do I have the opportunity? I certainly had the desire, and experience indicated that I could do it. It was the opportunity that was in question. So I reasoned that if I applied the seat of the pants to the seat of the chair each day and wrote, it would all work out, and in spite of the warning in Ecclesiastes that "of making many books there is no end," I went ahead.

I have several cartoons stuck on the wall where I write. In one, a smug-looking postman is handing an envelope to an irritated writer who says, "I appreciate the advice, but I think I'll stick with it for awhile longer if you don't mind." Another one is even more pointed. A sign on the door says EDITOR, and a man behind the desk is telling a visitor, "I think you should trade your word processor for a trash compactor." After five months of sending out pieces of a manuscript and waiting for a reply, the cartoons were no longer funny. So when I received an offer of another half-time job to complement the one I had, I accepted it as God's will. I had had my chance to write. Now it seemed that the window of opportunity had slammed shut. I had to move on to something else.

Several weeks after I began the new job, however, I received a contract with a request to complete the book in four months. I thought for a long time about God's timing, and I imagined all sorts of reasons for it. It was his timing, I was sure of that, but to this day

I don't understand it. What I do understand is that it is a call to faith, one of many such daily calls. Sin clouds my vision like dirt or ice on my windshield. I know the road is straight ahead and someday I'll see it clearly. I'll know the master plan. For now I know only what God tells me I need to know.

Four Things I Know for Sure

God Isn't Done with Me Yet

Finding God in everything is not a one-time event, like conversion or a trip to the Holy Land. It's a journey, a way of life, an ongoing discovery of a connection between the ordinary and the Eternal. However, I had lived many years as a believer before I truly discovered the implications of this particular truth for my life.

I still have the big, black Bible I bought as a freshman in college in the fall of 1950. It's a leather-bound, King James Version with notes by a famous Bible scholar named C. I. Scofield. I had seen several other students carry one around, and it seemed to be the thing to do. I had watched some of those students very carefully for several months. They had something else besides Bibles that intrigued me, something that set them apart from other Christians I had known, something I liked and envied.

Slowly I learned that these young men who had become my friends had a relationship with God that I didn't have. While I believed each tenet of the creed, I really didn't know God. I had an intellectual belief in a God who had died on a cross for the world, not a personal tie to a God who had taken my sins to that cross and died for me.

I was living at home that first semester, in a big, old, drafty house with peeling paint and creaky floors and a coal-burning furnace. One night I took my books and Bible to the bedroom to study, but the thought that something was wrong in my life persisted. Something was missing, something that tied the creed together and made sense of life. I took the big Scofield Bible and opened it to the verse in Revelation that says, "Here I am! I stand at the door and knock. If anyone hears my voice and opens the door, I will come in and eat with him, and he with me" (NIV). It had been explained to me that this was Jesus talking, and the door he referred to was the door of my life. So I knelt on the cold, wooden floor beside an iron bedstead and prayed something like this: "Lord, I believe this promise you have made to come into my life and live in me. That's what I want. I'll take you at your Word."

I couldn't have explained to you in theological terms what happened to me that evening. But I mark that as the beginning of a new life and a new relationship to God. It was also the beginning of a long journey. God began to work in my life that night, and as it says in the Scriptures, he "will carry it on to completion until the day of Christ Jesus" (Phil. 1:6).

Many years passed before I began in earnest to search for God in each routine and seemingly meaningless event of the day. Only in the past few years have I begun to discover—and that only in small glimpses—what de Caussade calls "the sacrament of the present moment." And I pray now for the grace to make this a way of life, to see each day as part of a long journey with God as my traveling companion and guide. And as I do, I will say four things with certainty:

First, trouble will come. Life is difficult. I must mourn as well as dance. For our first family vacation, Mary and I chose one of North Carolina's barrier islands and a comfortable cottage right on the beach. We both looked forward to long walks in the sand by the water, and on one particular night a balmy breeze and a nearly full moon made it a romantic setting. But as we walked, the tension was so great you could have plucked the air and played the old gospel song, "The Fight Is On." Holidays can be minefields for any normal family, but we were a blended family in its early stages, and it was dynamite. And, to change the metaphor, like the hurricane that had chased us off the island the day after we arrived, this tempest took us by surprise.

Several days before, Hurricane Bob had forced us inland where six of us took the only shelter we could find—one room in a hotel. For hours we watched the weather channel, played Trivial Pursuit, read all sixteen pages of the local paper, and finally pushed pillows and mattresses around so that everyone could have a bunk for the night. In spite of so much enforced togetherness in a cramped space, the occasion had remained amazingly conflict-free, so when two evenings after our return to the beach Mary and I began to argue, it caught us off guard. As it turned out, we probably had more strained exchanges about the kids in the next few days than we had had in any of our fifty-seven weeks of marriage.

During seven months of courtship, we had had hardly a word of disagreement. In fact we often laughed and told friends we hadn't had our first fight yet. This might have worried some marriage counselors who believe couples need to learn to fight constructively, and the sooner the better. So be it! We weren't about to start a fire so we could learn how to put it out.

Like most couples in love, we wanted to believe love conquers all problems, disagreements, moods, imperfections. Our love, strong and pure, would carry us successfully through wars, hurricanes, family games of Trivial Pursuit, or whatever beset us. We knew better, of course. And all the while we counted the days of courtship without a harsh word we wondered when the first one would come.

We've had them now, I can assure you, although we're not the kind of volatile couple that handles conflicts with a lot of shouting and door slamming, and we try not to let the ill winds of misunderstanding build up into one catastrophic cyclone. That night on the beach was not our first fight, and we managed to return from that walk much closer to each other than when we started, having found God there. Since then we've also had minor mishaps, sickness, suffering, major disappointments—the normal storms of life. We've had no major hurricanes that have forced us inland, no tragic accidents or life-threatening illnesses or losses, but we know those could come. But one thing we do know, that just as certain as hurricanes come to North Carolina, from time to time black clouds will hover over our lives.

The second thing I can be sure of in this long journey is I'm not in control. God has reminded me of that in different ways but none more forcefully than through the life of my friend Jim. I was reading in my study early one Saturday morning when the phone rang, and when I answered, I heard a gravelly voice croak, "Ron!"

I shuddered! I had expected the call, and while I knew who it was, I couldn't believe that feeble cry belonged to him. They had evacuated him on a stretcher by air ambulance from Kenya to a hospital close to my home, with an unknown intestinal problem. After two operations and three weeks in bed, this six-foot, two-inch model of midlife health had lost forty pounds and gained a chart full of aches and pains and undiagnosed ailments.

"How are you doing?" (I asked the obvious as a way of saying, "I care!") But that cracked, hoarse voice had revealed it all.

"Ron, God is teaching me about weakness and humility," he confessed.

I knew I had a lot to learn about my own inability to control the people and events around me, and in the next few days as I visited him, I wondered if I could learn those lessons at arm's length. Could Jim's experience rub off on me? Or would God allow me in time to pass again, and perhaps again, through the dark valley in which Jim now dwelled, to teach me that simple lesson?

We don't consider weakness or the admission thereof a virtue in our culture. We worship the god of strength, and we cultivate the perception of it. I've always found the strutting, bicep-flexing stereotype of machismo quite comical, yet I exercise and diet and groom and maintain an appearance of having life under control. I want to believe and convince the world I have it all together, rather than show off my shortcomings.

How different is God's way. I "prefer to find my joy and pride in the very things that are my weakness,"

Paul writes to the Christians in Corinth (2 Cor. 12:9 NEB). In fact he lists his shortcomings in bold type on his resume. "God's power is made perfect in my weakness," he writes, "for when I am weak, then I am strong."

This may not be one of the great mysteries of the Christian faith—like the Trinity or the resurrection—but it is awesome and marvelous to consider. The more I have, the less I depend on him. And as I grasp how truly poor and needy I am, then I can let God's power come to full strength in me.

That's a lot easier to do, Jim will agree, when you lie in bed looking up to heaven because you don't have the strength to get up. But how quickly we forget! If I can meet my deadlines, pay my mortgage, keep the grass cut and the car running, feed my family, get to church, and put in two and a half hours a week of community service, I tend to believe I have everything under control. I sing, "Praise God from whom all blessings flow," yet I conclude I must have done something right to achieve such a state of well-being.

One summer while driving across Missouri, Clint and I stopped at a large amusement park. He rode those big, mean machines that spin, shake, bump, drop, and generally terrify anyone over forty but thrill a twelve-year-old. While he was on one of those, I wandered around and came across what appeared to be a harmless looking ride. So I stepped into one of the cars only to find myself on a "junior-sized" roller coaster and soon out of control. For several long minutes I realized I had to completely trust the fiendish, and possibly sadistic, inventor who designed the contraption.

It's scary for us to let go, to admit as I was forced to do on that roller coaster that we have little power to command the forces that impinge on our life. But watching God work helps to increase the trust I have that he is in control, not only of the world but of every detail of my life.

And that leads me to the third certainty: many times I will fail. I am easily distracted. I often get my priorities wrong. My vision is clouded and my hearing is hindered. I forget the goal. I don't stop to wait on God, nor do I live like a son of the Father in heaven. I live long periods of time as an orphan, and when I do, I invariably break one or another of God's laws. It's my nature, of course. My pastor, John Hall, often begins to pray by saying, "Lord, we're a mess." I resonate with that. It touches a deep chord of truth in me. But the point is the more I find God in the ordinary and observe him at work around me, the fewer the falls—and the easier the landing.

The fourth certainty is that I will find forgiveness and get up and go on. God will wipe up the mess I've made of things, take me by the hand, and set me back on the right path. God will complete the work he began. He has promised. As Clint and I wandered the fairway of the amusement park that summer day, we came by a booth where a young woman boasted that for two bucks she'd guess my age by two years. If she missed, I'd win a prize.

Just another way to throw away two bucks, I thought, and kept walking. But Clint urged me to try it. When I balked, he persisted. Perhaps vanity made me do it, although I fully believed the young woman would see my gray hair and liver spots and know in a flash I was eligible for a senior citizen discount at most fine restaurants and motels.

So I stepped into the little square chalked on the asphalt that she called "my office," while she went around behind me and wrote a number on a piece of paper. "Now, sir, tell us how old you are," she instructed me confidently. "Sixty," I answered, and sheepishly she showed me the "53" she had written on her paper. My prize: a porcelain coffee mug that advertises the St. Louis Zoo, which probably sells for $1.25 wholesale.

It may be impossible at a moment's glance for any of us to see the work that God is doing in us. Like the woman on the fairway, the casual observer sees the outside, the smooth skin or the wrinkles, the muscles or the flab, the well constructed physique or the bent and deformed body. And all too often we make judgments from that. I got a big kick out of fooling the expert age-teller. I feel a lot closer to the age she saw in me than what appears on my driver's license.

Physical appearance, however, has nothing to do with the state of one's soul or spiritual health. I may run a marathon next year, or I may be in a rocking chair. I may still fool the self-styled experts as well as my friends, or I may be bent over and not able to see well enough to find my ear trumpet. Neither state will reflect what's inside. You can count on this, however, that God will be working in me to finish what he started. It won't be completed on earth. This is still a fallen world. But someday, with a great "ta ta ta da" on a trumpet and a flourish possible only in heaven, I will become like him and will see him face to face.

Do You Know What You've Got?

Beginning a Life of Watching God Work

Don't it always seem to go that you don't
  know what you've got 'til it's gone.
They paved Paradise and put in a parking lot.

Joni Mitchell

Not too long ago I worshiped in a place where Christians have gathered for more than a thousand years. I sat in the stalls of Christ Church Cathedral on the banks of the Thames in Oxford, England, while the twenty-eight-voice male choir rang praises up the medieval walls where English kings and queens once worshiped. John Locke and W. H. Auden, among other greats, studied here, and a college math teacher named Charles Dodgson wrote *Alice in Wonderland* under the pseudonym of Lewis Carroll. Earlier I had walked through this city of spires and massive stone buildings, some from the twelfth and thirteenth centuries, and had come upon Magdalen College where C. S. Lewis studied and taught.

It all gave me a fresh sense of the historical nature of our faith in an age that would cast the past into the rubbish bin of irrelevance. In the church in which I worship at home, we sing old hymns as well as new songs of praise, and we recite ancient creeds repeated for centuries by Christians the world over. We do this to affirm our connection to the church universal.

The sense of history instilled in that place also reminded me that my story is not unique. Not only is renewal a common experience in the Christian life, but the revelation of God working in and around us and the enrichment that brings has been repeated in countless souls for two millennia. How many times, I wonder, has God met a believer who was only ambling along, seemingly making little progress in the journey? How often has he picked up a wanderer and set him back on the path? How many Christians have opened their eyes one day to see God in a new way and recognized the divine working in both the large and small events of their lives?

God used a devastating loss, followed by acts of mercy and grace, to start me on a new phase of my life in him. But it doesn't have to be that way. Your life may be moving uneventfully over a smooth sea.

It may appear that things can't get any better. Or you may have a nagging awareness that they can. Or, even still, you may be fully aware that God has something more in mind than the routine of spiritual exercises (or the lack thereof) into which you have fallen.

I pray that this book may be the catalyst that God will use in your life to begin a similar journey. You may have a long history as a Christian believer or you may have just begun the journey. You may be a teenager, a mother of five, a retired businessman, or a seminary graduate. No matter. I don't believe God discriminates by age or position or experience. For reasons far beyond our capability to discern he nudges different ones at different times, and he uses various events to get our attention. May he use these very words to get yours and accomplish his purpose in your life.

For most of this book I have used the first person in reflecting on my experiences: This is what happened, and this is what God said to me. But all along I have assumed you will apply the stories and lessons as they fit your circumstance. Now I no longer want to make any assumptions. I want to invite you to begin the same walk I have described here. Begin to look for God in "the smallest and most ordinary things, as well as in the greatest." See him in the trivial as well as the traumatic, in the grandiose as well as the routine. He is there as you receive great honors or enjoy good things. And he is there as you park the car or brush your teeth. Converse with him, enjoy his walk with you. Know that nothing escapes his notice, he is never off duty. Do this and you will discover, as de Caussade writes, "a rare and sublime faith."

At the same time I want to make a confession. In recent days I have not always known the same deep hunger for God that I experienced when I began this book. This book began in solitude in a time of heartache. I sought the solitude because there I found the only relief for the loneliness that permeated my soul. In fact, I even delved into the literature of meditation to understand the concept of solitude. If the balm was applied most effectively in silence before God, I wanted all I could get.

Now, however, the wound has healed, and God, in his wisdom and grace, has granted me family, health, fellowship, comfort, a place of service, and blessings too many to count. And therein is the greatest danger I face: How do I maintain that sense of desperation and hunger for God that arose in meaner circumstances? Without the soul distress that drove me to him just a few years ago, how will I maintain the art of watching God work and the soul stretching that results from it? In simple language, what is it that keeps me—and you—close to God in the good times?

The answer is as clear to me now as it was then. It is in solitude. Quietness. Waiting and listening, turning down the boom box of the world and turning up my spiritual hearing aid. Seeking before anything and everything the face and the voice of God in long encounters with him.

I like the lines Joni Mitchell sings: "Don't it always seem to go that you don't know what you've got 'til it's gone." (As I write I can hear the high, thin wail of her voice.) The kingdom of God is like that. We don't fully understand what we've got. We hold a priceless treasure but don't recognize its full value. The man who found a treasure hidden in the field went and sold everything he had and bought that field. That, the Lord told his disciples, is like the kingdom of heaven. While there is time, gaze on it. Begin to watch God work in his marvelous way in your life.

Epilogue

My Secret Life as a Bibliophile

I am a self-confessed and unashamed bibliophile. A good book to me is a thing of beauty, if not a security blanket. Until I arrive in heaven, few things will give me more pleasure than time spent in libraries and bookstores or curled up on the couch absorbed by the stories and ideas between two covers.

I've always believed that anything I wanted or needed to know I could find between two covers, and I found the proof for that years ago as I walked up Charing Cross Road in London. London itself is a mecca for book lovers of all types. If you want first editions, for example, or want to tread where Charles Dickens trod, go to Southeran's of Sackville Street, just off of Picadilly Circus. If you want children's books or maps or used paperbacks, you'll find shops to suit your fancy.

For me it all culminated as I walked up this busy street in the center of London's famed West End.

Jammed between theaters and cinemas and travel agencies are dusty shops of rare and not-so-rare books, as well as modern chain stores with tables piled high with remainders. And at the head of it all is Foyles, a five-story warehouse with high, narrow stacks of books from Abalone to Zwingli, stacked in disorderly piles. I've lost myself in Foyles for an afternoon or a morning on more than one occasion.

It is little wonder that books have played a very large part in shaping my life and especially in guiding my spiritual development in recent years. I've already alluded to many and to their authors, but I want to give credit to a number of writers who have influenced my thinking and whose ideas I have freely borrowed for this book. I mention them here not just out of appreciation, but to introduce them as friends with whom I have had long and enjoyable conversations and with whom I would feel already well acquainted if they showed up on my doorstep.

I don't pretend that this is the definitive list of books for spiritual growth. This is just my personal list and only a few of my favorites.

- Dietrich Bonhoeffer—*A Testament to Freedom.* Bonhoeffer was a German pastor and theologian who resisted the Nazis, was imprisoned, then executed in 1945 only weeks before the end of the war. This volume contains his essential writings, including many of his letters from prison. (Edited by Geffrey B. Kelly & F. Burton Nelson, San Francisco: HarperCollins, 1990.)

- Frederick Buechner—*Now and Then—A Memoir of Vocation*. Buechner is a great prose stylist, easy and enjoyable to read. But he is also honest and insightful as he relates incidents from his own life. (San Francisco: HarperCollins, 1983.)
- Jean-Pierre de Caussade—*The Sacrament of the Present Moment*. Much of the inspiration for what I have written here came from this eighteenth-century French priest. I read this book slowly, a sentence or paragraph at a time, and found it filled with gems that have provided many hours of fruitful meditation. (San Francisco: Harper & Row, 1982.)
- Annie Dillard—*Pilgrim at Tinker Creek*. Dillard's insights into nature and life, combined with her creative use of language, make this a delightful book to read over and over.(San Francisco: HarperCollins, 1988.)
- Richard Foster—*Celebration of Discipline*. This has become almost a classic without the benefit of age. I've read it several times and go back to it often. (San Francisco: HarperCollins, 1978.)
- Richard Foster—*Prayer: Finding the Heart's True Home*. It is evident that Richard knows about prayer both from reading and research and from

experience. His classification of the kinds of prayer and his quotes from many sources made it especially rich for me. (San Francisco: HarperCollins, 1992.)

- Thomas R. Kelly—*A Testament of Devotion.* Richard Foster, through his writings, introduced me to Thomas Kelly and to this small book. Kelly takes up the theme of the continual presence of God but puts his own inspiring twist to it. (San Francisco: Harper & Brothers, 1941.)
- Brother Lawrence—*Practicing the Presence of God.* This is truly a classic, a little book you could read in an hour but will want to spend much longer with. (Springdale, Pa.: Whitaker House, 1982.)
- C. S. Lewis—*Mere Christianity.* This is a defense of the Christian faith and possibly the most well-known of Lewis's books. I enjoy dipping in from time to time not only because Lewis is such a fine writer and a brilliant apologist but because the genuine person comes through as he writes. (New York: Macmillan, 1953.)
- Malcolm Muggeridge—*Something Beautiful for God.* The personal response of a famous journalist to Mother Teresa. It's one man's portrait of the saint, plus some of her writings. (Garden City, N.Y.: Image Books, 1977.)
- Andrew Murray—*Humility.* Gently but firmly Murray exposes the buried pride that prompts

so many of our responses and shapes so much of our soul. (Springdale, Pa.: Whitaker House, 1982.)

- Andrew Murray—*Waiting on God.* Murray was a Scottish pastor in the early part of this century. This book is both an inspirational treasure and down-to-earth biblical exposition. (Springdale, Pa.: Whitaker House, 1982.)
- Henri J. M. Nouwen—What do I say about Henri Nouwen, except that I have read everything he has written that I could get my hands on? It is not that he is Dutch and that I, having lived in the Netherlands for a time, have an inordinate love of all things Dutch. Nor that, being of a similar age, I identify with some of the stages of life through which he appears to be passing. More, it is his vulnerability combined with spiritual insights through which the Spirit has spoken to me in a loud voice. I list here just four of my favorite books (and an article) by this wise and humble priest:

  The Way of the Heart. (New York: Ballantine Books, 1981.)

  Reaching Out. (New York: Image Books, 1975.)

  The Return of the Prodigal Son. (New York: Doubleday, 1992.)

  The Road to Daybreak. (New York: Doubleday, 1988.)

"The Duet of the Holy Spirit: When Mourning and Dancing Are One." *The New Oxford Review*, June 1992.

- M. Scott Peck—*The Road Less Traveled.* It would not do this book credit to call it a psychological self-help book, although it is very much that. It is also a spiritual book to which I have returned many times for my edification. (New York: Simon & Schuster, 1978.)
- Eugene Peterson—*A Long Obedience in the Same Direction*. Like Andrew Murray's book, this is both inspirational and biblical exposition. Except that Peterson is a contemporary with the ability to express ideas in very clear terms. On top of that, you know as you read that this pastor-turned-seminary professor writes from experience. (Downers Grove, Ill.: InterVarsity Press, 1980.)
- *The Message*, a paraphrase of the New Testament by Eugene Peterson. The language is so fresh that as I read I kept saying to myself, I don't remember reading that in the Bible. (Colorado Springs: Navpress, 1993.)
- John Sherrill—*The Hiding Place*. This is the story of Corrie ten Boom, one of the dearest old saints you could ever hope to meet. After her release from a prison camp in World War II, God gave her a ministry of reconciliation. (Grand Rapids: Fleming H. Revell, 1988.)

- A. W. Tozer—*The Pursuit of God.* A.W. Tozer was still alive when I first moved to Chicago in 1959, and I deeply regret I never met him or heard him preach. Not only was he a plain-spoken preacher and writer, I gather from reading this book that he was also "the genuine article." (Camp Hill, Pa.: Christian Publications, Inc., 1982.)
- John Wesley—*The Nature of Holiness*. Wesley grows on you. His zeal and his total commitment are evident, and his discourses on the nature of the Christian life are brilliant. (Minneapolis: Bethany House Publishers, 1988.)

A Little Help from My Friends

I get by with a little help from my friends.
John Lennon & Paul McCartney

Scores of people, many of whom I've long forgotten, have influenced me in the more than forty years of my Christian life. But this story takes place in the last six years, and I must mention several, without whose friendship I would have a different story to write.

Mary, my wife, above all, has encouraged me, prayed for me, taught me through both word and deed, and endured my long absences—in body and spirit—while I completed this manuscript. I am deeply in debt to her for her godly example and her faithful support.

Doug Wallace, my friend of many years, has always been there to pray and laugh with me, to share his own needs and struggles, to talk about God, to cry or relax or simply enjoy life itself with me. Wordsmith though I profess to be, I can find none that adequately express my love for him.

Jim Nash, likewise, in his friendship to me, has modeled Christ's unconditional love as closely as I ever expect to find it on earth. His single-minded faith and desire to know and please God have been a constant example to me.

Skip Ryan was both my pastor and my friend at the beginning of this odyssey. His wise use of his own spiritual gifts, plus his gentle spirit and genuine love, did much to move me on the road I have written about.

David Turner offered many good insights as well as prayers and gave willingly of his time and interest as I struggled with the shape of this book. I'm deeply grateful for him.

Bob Osborne has encouraged me often with his persistent friendship, his pursuit of holiness, and his unquenchable spirit. I'm constantly challenged by his life and his quiet service.

John Hall has been my pastor a little more than a year, but often in this short period the Spirit has used his messages and his life to inspire me. I believe he will continue to be an instrument of God in my sanctification, as well as a friend to enjoy.

Not much in this book except my experience is original, so I hereby acknowledge my debt to a long parade of unnamed saints and sinners who in some way have touched my life and made this work possible.

Ronald E. Wilson is executive director of the Evangelical Press Association and editor of the book division of Overseas Missionary Fellowship (OMF). He has also served as editor of *Campus Life* magazine, as a missionary journalist in Europe, and as a freelance editor and consultant for Christian organizations. Ron lives with his wife, Mary, in Earlysville, Virginia.